3 1

HISTORIC  SCOTLAND

SCOTLAND'S
CASTLES

The Castle of Old Wick, perched on a narrow promontory thrusting out from the Caithness coast into the North Sea. Built possibly by Earl Harald Maddadson of Orkney in the twelfth century, the lonely tower, known locally as 'The Old Man of Wick', reminds us that in the Middle Ages much of northern and western Scotland, including the Northern and Western Isles and great swathes of the mainland too, lay outside the realm of Scotland, under the nominal control of the kings of Norway.

HISTORIC SCOTLAND

SCOTLAND'S CASTLES

CHRIS TABRAHAM

B T BATSFORD / HISTORIC SCOTLAND

First published 2005
© Chris Tabraham 1997, 2005

The right of Chris Tabraham to be identified as Author of this work has been asserted by him in accordance with the Copyright, Designs and Patents Act 1988.

Volume © B T Batsford

ISBN 0 7134 8943 X

A CIP catalogue record for this book is available from the British Library.

Printed in Singapore

for the publisher
B T Batsford
The Chrysalis Building
Bramley Road
London W10 6SP
www.chrysalisbooks.co.uk

An imprint of Chrysalis Books Group plc

Contents

Introduction:

'Welcvm freindis'

On a cold winter's evening a few years ago, Jock Smith, a gap-toothed, bow-legged figure of a man, was preparing to lock up his premises for the night before making his way home. 'Auld Jock' was custodian for the Ministry of Public Building and Works of Threave Castle, the island fastness of the Black Douglases in the Galloway Dee. Having done his rounds of the grim, forbidding tower, he was about to put the heavy iron key into the lock when he heard a deep voice call out from the bowels of the building: 'Jock, Jock,' the disembodied voice pronounced, 'this is Archibald the Grim; an' it's just thee and me here noo.' Quick as a flash, Jock replied: 'O no it's not, ya bugger; I'm off!' In an instant the door was locked and Jock was rowing like a man possessed across the icy waters of the Dee to the safety of the far bank.

Those of us who have had the good fortune to visit Threave Island will have every sympathy for Jock; I suspect that we would all have done likewise had we been in his shoes – the ruined castle has a haunting quality, enough to make the hairs on the back of your neck stand on end. I know I would have turned and run, but I also know that I would have bitterly regretted it for the rest of my days. Who among us has not made a secret wish to go back in time, just for a short while, to see for ourselves exactly what life was like at a particular moment? What I would have given to have spent that winter's evening in the company of Black Archibald, third earl of the house of Douglas, lord of Galloway, scourge of the English and arguably the most powerful nobleman in the land at his death at Threave on Christmas Eve 1400. What he could have told me about castles and castle life; and what a book I might have written! As things are, this book of mine will just have to take its place alongside the others on the subject written by folk without the benefit of time travel.

Scotland is a land full of castles. Those two great Victorian 'castle buffs' David MacGibbon and Thomas Ross included 769 castles in their pioneering five-volume epic *The castellated and domestic architecture of Scotland from the twelfth to the eighteenth century*, published just over a century ago – and they confined their coverage to just stone ones. Today's computer in the National Monuments Record of Scotland holds thousands of entries covering all types of medieval fortified sites, whether of stone or timber. Clearly, my book cannot include them all, nor would I wish it to. A simple gazetteer would not even begin to reveal the fascinating and complex story of Scotland's castles.

Scotland is also a country as rich as any other in its variety of castles. People in medieval times referred to them by a befuddling variety of names, among them *castrum, fortalicium, turris, manerium, mansio, domus, locus, palatium, capitale* and *principale messuagium*. I am sure that Black Archibald would have been able to enlighten me as to their respective meanings. However, all we can say today is that Scotland's castles came in all shapes and sizes – mighty castles royal, impressive seats of the great and grand, fortified homes of the middling sort and poky dwellings of those on the bottom rung of the landholding ladder. Clearly, this book should try to embrace them all, and I hope that it does. Only by looking at the Scottish fortified house in all its manifestations can we begin to appreciate the whole picture.

There is an old adage: 'An Englishman's home is his castle.' Perhaps we should create another: 'A Scotsman's castle is his home.' In a way, this would be the more accurate, for the medieval castle dominated Scottish life for far longer than was the case south of the Border.

What is more, we today have come to see castles as high-status sites, associating their ruins with the high-born in society. But this is to overlook just how many Scots from all walks of life, freeman or serf, town-dweller or countryman, were dependent on the castle; it could be their home, their place of work, their place of worship, their rent office, their army barracks, their law court, their prison, their hotel, their place of entertainment – even their place of execution. As an archaeologist, I am fascinated by this human aspect of the Scottish castle, and this is what I attempt to cover in this book.

And so, as a carved lintel above the front door into Otterston Castle, Fife, declares:

1

Castles in the land: the twelfth century

When the queen heard this [news of her husband's death] she shrived, and devoutly took the Communion in church; and, commending herself unto God in prayer, she gave back her saintly soul to heaven, in the Castle of Maidens [Edinburgh] on 16th November, the fourth day after the king. Whereupon Donald Bane, the king's brother, having heard of her death, invaded the kingdom, at the head of a numerous band, and in hostile-wise besieged the castle, where he knew the king's rightful and lawful heirs were. But, forasmuch as that spot is in itself strongly fortified by nature, he thought that the gates only should be guarded, because it was not easy to see any other entrance or outlet. When those who were within understood this, they brought down her holy body by a postern on the western side.

1 Edinburgh Castle Rock from the south, with the River Forth in the background. Recent archaeological excavations have shown that the Rock was inhabited at least as early as the late Bronze Age (about 900 BC).

Origins

The moving story of the saintly Queen Margaret's death in Edinburgh Castle (**1**) in November 1093, while in mourning for her beloved husband King Malcolm III, appears at first sight to give us our first mention of a Scottish castle in the country's annals. On further inspection, however, we discover that the author of the account, the chronicler John of Fordun, was writing in the later fourteenth century, almost three centuries after the tragic events. The near-contemporary recording of the event by Bishop Turgot in his *Life of St Margaret* makes no mention of a castle, let alone one called the 'Castle of Maidens' at Edinburgh.

The nature of Queen Margaret's residence, whether at Edinburgh, Dunfermline or elsewhere, is only glimpsed at in Turgot's *Life*. He writes of churches and oratories, of private chambers, and of royal halls big enough to hold '300 poor people'. But nowhere does he mention castles. His descriptions could just as equally fit the remains of Dark-Age buildings recently excavated on the rocky summits at Cruggleton (Wigtownshire) and Dundonald (Ayrshire), or beside the cliff-edge in Dunbar (East Lothian), and on the slope of wind-swept Doon Hill, a short distance inland from there. So were there castles in the land in Queen Margaret's day?

There were certainly castles south of the Border in England and Wales and across the North Sea on the mainland of Europe in her day. The origin of castles remains a mystery, but the debate need not concern us unduly for by the time castles appeared in Scotland they had developed a recognized form and function. Castles were essentially fortified residences of lordship, the homes of those who held land in return for military service. They might differ in size and scale according to the rank of those building and occupying them, and royal castles in particular served a heightened political and public role; but all castles essentially performed the same purpose.

It is just possible that Queen Margaret was personally acquainted with the castle form through her residence in England prior to her flight to Scotland in about 1070. Her husband Malcolm must surely have been familiar with them through his various forays into England. In 1092, the year the English king William Rufus captured Carlisle from the Scots and began to build a castle there, Malcolm journeyed to Gloucester Castle where he was snubbed by Rufus. Infuriated, Malcolm returned home and in the following year led his fourth and final raid into northern England. His ensuing death at the hand of Arkil Morel, one of Rufus's Norman knights, which led so soon after to Queen Margaret's demise, occurred within a bow-shot of Alnwick Castle.

Despite this intermittent friction between Malcolm's Scotland and Norman England, the two countries shared in a reasonably peaceful coexistence. This was further cemented after Margaret and Malcolm's deaths by arranged marriages and other amicable relationships between the two royal houses. In 1100 their elder daughter, Matilda, actually became queen of England when she wed William I's youngest son, Henry I; the Conqueror's invasion of Scotland in 1072, when he got as far as the River Tay and received King Malcolm's homage, must have been a fading memory at the wedding reception!

The increasing contact between the Scots and their new aristocratic neighbours inevitably brought the former into contact with all manner of French customs and ways. (The 'Norman' conquerors of England were drawn from a wider field than just Normandy, including regions like Brittany and the Pas de Calais.) We know that the temptation to imitate some of these habits was irresistible. Indeed, Donald Bane's seizure of the throne immediately after Queen Margaret's death, mentioned in Fordun's account, was said to have been motivated by his burning desire to rid the country of these incomers and their alien ways. These certainly included the introduction of mailed knights; even King Macbeth in the early 1050s had had Normans in his retinue. But did these French ways also include the building of castles?

It is difficult not to see them including this most visible form of aristocratic power, although the evidence is scanty to say the least and no castle site has yet been positively identified as dating from this period. King Edgar, the second of Margaret and Malcolm's six sons (and the one who broke the tragic news of his father's death to his mother), certainly received substantial help from William Rufus in his successful attempt to overthrow Donald Bane in 1097; and among those who came north in that year to serve him was an English baron called Robert, son of Godwin. Following the victory, Edgar rewarded Robert with an estate in Lothian, close to the English Border, where the latter endeavoured to build a castle.

This may be an isolated incident, the exception perhaps to prove the rule that castles were not yet part of Scottish society or a feature in her landscape. But given the close ties between the Canmores and the Conqueror's dynasty, and given also the undoubted familiarity of the Scots with the new-fangled fighting ways of the Normans, it is difficult to resist the notion that the castle might have become a little more firmly embedded in the fabric of Scotland prior to the time of King David I in the second quarter of the twelfth century.

There is some evidence that King Alexander I (1107–24) was beginning to rely less on foreign mercenaries and more on those who would settle permanently and offer military service in return for their lands. The building of castles would be the logical consequence of such a policy. Even if the incomers were not building castles, it would be surprising if the king himself, having seen the new strongholds built by the English crown at the likes of Carlisle and Newcastle, was not persuaded to follow suit. One wonders what might have stood atop the rocky crags of Stirling or Edinburgh in the early twelfth century.

David – king of the castle

King David I, the youngest of Margaret and Malcolm's six sons, succeeded his brother Alexander in 1124 (**2**). He had, however, been in effective control of southern Scotland from as early as 1113. It was during the time of David, 'that most vigorous and courteous of kings', that the process of settling an immigrant aristocracy on Scotland's soil began in earnest, a development that would continue long after his death in 1153, under the encouragement of his two grandsons who succeeded him, Malcolm IV 'the Maiden' and William 'the Lion'. The process was not completed until William's demise in 1214. A verse inserted into the *Chronicle of Melrose* for the year 1153 leaves us in no doubt about his contribution:

> David was king in Scotland for twenty-nine years,
> Warily discerning what was provident;
> After he had fortified the kingdom with castles and arms,
> The king died, an old man, at Carlisle.

Fordun himself proudly proclaimed: 'He it is that has decked thee [Scotland] with castles and towns, and with lofty towers.'

David was born in Dunfermline about 1080. While still in his teens, he travelled south into England for his sister Matilda's wedding to Henry I. There he remained for the next decade and more, attending at the English court and observing at first hand French ways and customs. He became one of Henry's barons, and in 1113 he married Maud, a rich widow, thereby becoming lord of the extensive Honour of Huntingdon, in the East Midlands.

Shortly afterwards, he returned to the land of his birth with a Norman education, a Norman wife and a large English estate full of Norman knights. Life in Scotland was never going to be quite the same again.

David's legacy for Scotland, continued by his grandsons, was immense. He reorganized the church and introduced the new reformed monastic orders; he established towns and built mints for the striking of coin; he introduced a new type of sheriffdom based on the Norman model; and he forced the pace on the 'feudalizing' of Scotland, encouraging newcomers to settle in the land and cajoling native lords to adapt to the new ways. One thing is certain, it must have been 'boom time' for the construction industry, and alongside the new cathedrals, monasteries, parish churches and towns arose the castles, the most potent symbol of the new order in Scotland.

2 David I, King of Scots (1124–1153), with his grandson and successor (right), King Malcolm IV (1153–65); a decorated initial from a charter granted to Kelso Abbey, Roxburghshire, in 1159.

Castles for kings, barons and knights

There were essentially two categories of castle introduced into Scotland during the course of the twelfth century: royal castles and castles built by tenants of the crown – barons and knights, holding their land in return for military service.

By 1200 there were royal castles as far apart as Berwick-upon-Tweed, hard by the English Border, Ayr in the west and Dunskeath in the north. These were intended to perform a variety of functions. They were primarily, of course, the fortified residences of the monarchy, though the royal family never dwelt in them permanently but travelled around the kingdom, overseeing the nation's affairs, consuming their rents which were normally paid in kind, or simply pursuing their leisure interests. While in residence, the royal family ruled from them, entertained at them, and lived and died in them. Prince Henry, David's only son and heir, tragically died in the royal castle at Peebles (**3**) in 1152, King David himself passed away at Carlisle Castle in the following year, Malcolm breathed his last at Jedburgh Castle in 1165 and William his last at Stirling Castle in 1214.

In addition to their use as occasional residences, royal castles were important as permanent centres of national government. Each in effect became the regional headquarters of the royal administrative unit – the shire or sheriffdom – whose chief administrator was the sheriff. The sheriff usually served also as the constable, or keeper of the castle, being responsible for its garrisoning, provisioning and maintenance. He had an official residence in the castle and held his court of justice in its great hall. Royal castles were thus law courts and prisons as well as residences.

The incoming aristocracy, and the native nobility who embraced the new order, also built castles. There were several rungs on the landholding ladder, and no doubt their fortified residences reflected this gradation. At the top were the magnates, who moved in much the same circle as the king himself; quite a number must have been his close personal friends. They were expected to control and administer their large estates and from them draw the necessary military strength required by the crown.

Typical of the incoming magnates was Robert de Brus, ancestor of King Robert the Bruce, who was granted the vast lordship of Annandale, adjacent to the English Border, in 1124 in return for the service of ten knights. De Brus was already lord of Cleveland, in England, but his roots reached back to Normandy, to the village of Brix in the Cotentin. The castle that Robert de Brus built beside the river at Annan (Dumfriesshire), which still partly exists, was not only his

fortified residence but the estate office and courthouse as well. An example of a native baron adapting to the changed regime is Earl Duncan of Fife, descended from the ancient mormaers who governed north of the Forth in the pre-feudal age. About 1136 Duncan was granted the earldom as a fief in return for military service, and he probably built the castle at Cupar (Fife) as a consequence of this new-found status.

4 Crookston Castle, Glasgow. The tower-house residence of Sir John Stewart of Darnley, built about 1400, stands within a ringwork defence dating to Sir Robert de Croc's time in the later twelfth century.

Magnates like Earl Duncan and Robert de Brus held their large lordships directly of the crown, but in order to meet their obligations they had to grant smaller parcels of land to others in return for service. These lower-ranking landholders were called knights, and they too were empowered to build castles. A good instance of this is the great feudal lordship of the Stewarts, concentrated chiefly in the west of the country and administered from their two principal castles at Renfrew and Dundonald. Only a comparatively small part of the lordship was held 'in demesne' (that is, retained in the lord's hands); the greater portion was let as subordinate fiefs to a variety of tenants and vassals, to men like Robert Croc, knight in Crookston (Glasgow), and Gilbert fitz Richer, knight in Tarbolton (Ayrshire). In each of these two fiefs there is an early castle (**4**).

The word 'demesne' survives today as 'mains', meaning the home farm of an estate cultivated by or for the proprietor. There are two other place-names, *ingleston* and *boreland*, which indicate the former existence of a castle, sometimes where there is no sign of one today. 'Ingleston' implies a settlement of incoming Englishmen in the area, while 'boreland' (sometimes 'bordland' or 'borland') referred to land that provided food for the lord's board or table. The farm-name of Borlum, on the high ground overlooking Urquhart Castle beside Loch Ness (Inverness-shire), is another corruption of the word.

The nature of castles – the literary evidence

What form then did these royal, baronial and knightly castles take? To help us in our quest we have the evidence from literature, from physical remains and from archaeological excavation.

There is a most wonderful love-story surviving from late twelfth-century Scotland, the *Roman de Fergus*, written by Guillaume le Clerc, identified by one authority (D.D.R. Owen in his translation *Fergus of Galloway, Knight of King Arthur,* 1991) as William Malveisin, a royal clerk who rose to become bishop of St Andrews in 1202. His romance, written perhaps in honour of the wedding of Roland of Galloway and Elena de Morville about the year 1170, is a novel worthy of the Booker prize! But despite being a work of fiction, with its predilection for tales of knightly derring-do, it paints for us today a unique and utterly fascinating picture of contemporary life in southern Scotland in this feudal age; and the picture is positively brimming with castles.

Our eponymous hero first encounters his true love, Galiena, at her uncle's castle, Liddel. We read of the bridge below the castle gate, of the stable where his horse was well supplied with hay and oats, and of the steps leading to the main hall, 'which was by no means small' and was furnished with couches and trestle-tables fashioned from ebony. A visit to present-day Liddel Castle, atop a steep cliff overlooking Liddel Water in deepest Liddesdale (Roxburghshire), is made the more rewarding with a copy of the *Roman de Fergus* to hand. It is a motte-and-bailey castle of somewhat eccentric form which in reality was the residence of Ranulf de Soules, who held the fief of Great Doddington (Northamptonshire) on King David's Honour of Huntingdon but who came north when the king granted him the lordship of Liddesdale and probably

5 Cruggleton Castle (centre background), near Garlieston, Wigtownshire, perched on a rocky cliff overlooking Wigtown Bay. The arch on the summit once formed part of the later medieval castle.

also the office of butler in his household. His nephew, the younger Ranulf, who succeeded him, became the stuff of legend in his own right as 'the wicked Lord Soules' who in 1207 was murdered in his castle at Liddel by his own servants.

Another absorbing insight from the *Roman* comes with Fergus's arrival at the 'Castle of the Dark Rock' high up in a mountain near Melrose, the 'wonderfully powerful stronghold' of a wicked giant whom Fergus, after a great deal of difficulty, overpowers and slays. Wearily he enters the castle where the dead giant's maidens 'provide for him a splendid, excellent bath' in the hall in the keep whose pillars hang 'with more than 1000 shields, hauberks, helmets, and all the gear for arming a knight'. We read also of a great hall separate from the keep, of an 'out-of-the-way cellar' wherein was a handsome horse, and of the drawbridge over the moat. At one point Fergus climbs to the upper floor of the keep and looks out of the window where he regards 'the tilled and the uncultivated land' of Lothian and the castle of Roxburgh (see **33**), where his lover is besieged. We subsequently discover that this castle has a square keep 'some 180 feet [55m] above the ground', a church and a postern gate.

But the most revealing insight comes at the very beginning of the tale as Fergus sets out on his travels from the home of his father, Soumillet:

> On the road out of Galloway, in a castle down a valley, lived a peasant of Pelande very close to the Irish Sea. He had his dwelling splendidly situated on a great rock, encircled by clay and wattle walls. The hill was topped by a tower that was not made of granite or limestone: its wall was built high of earth, with ramparts and battlements. The peasant was very well off to have such a handsome home by the sea. If he looked out he could see for thirty leagues all round. Nobody inside could feel threatened by any maker of siege equipment or from any assault, the rock being high and massive. Without a word of a lie, the peasant governed and held in his possession the whole of the country, which had been his for a very long time, and nobody could take it from him.

There are two likely candidates for Soumillet's residence, Kirklaugh Motte near Aṅwoth (Kirkcudbrightshire) and Cruggleton Castle near Garlieston (**5**). The latter is the more probable given its known association with the ancient lords of Galloway and we are fortunate that excavations have been carried out there recently to complement the evidence from literature (see page 22).

The nature of castles – the physical evidence

The most characteristic type of early castle is the motte. The word 'motta' literally means 'a clod of earth' but from the twelfth century it was used to denote a castle mound, whether natural or man-made. There are several depictions of mottes on the Bayeux Tapestry, that splendid late eleventh-century strip cartoon telling the story of the Norman conquest of England. One of them, that at Dol in Brittany, was the castle of the steward of the bishop of Dol, from whom our own Stewart dynasty of kings and queens was descended. Fieldwork in Scotland has identified about 300 of these

motte castles, of varying shape and size. To illustrate them I shall take two examples, each quite different, from opposite ends of the country.

The motte-and-bailey castle known as the Bass of Inverurie, in the Garioch of Aberdeenshire, is one of the best preserved in Scotland; it is also one of the best documented (**6**). It lies today in a quiet cemetery to the south-east of the present town, sandwiched between the rivers Urie and Don, but in its day it was the focal point of the burgh established by Earl David of Huntingdon in the late twelfth century; the burgh is on record by 1195 and the castle by 1199.

The motte and bailey suffered from some landscaping in the nineteenth century but it is essentially intact. It

6 The Bass of Inverurie, Aberdeenshire, the Scottish residence of Earl David of Huntingdon, and a classic example of a motte-and-bailey castle.

appears to be entirely man-made. The motte, the Bass itself, has the classic conical shape, like an upside-down pudding bowl, and rises some 15m (49ft) above the surrounding ground. The summit area is about 18m (59ft) in diameter. The bailey, or Little Bass, now shrouded in trees, is both smaller in height and in summit area. There is now no hint of the defensive ditch that doubtless encircled both motte and bailey, though excavation in the nineteenth century unearthed remains of an oak bridge.

Earl David (1152–1219), the builder of the Bass, was a member of the royal family, the youngest of King David's three grandsons. Following the death in 1165 of his eldest brother, Malcolm, David was heir apparent to the throne until 1198. He was thus among the élite in society, moving in the highest circles. During his thirties, Earl David acquired vast estates, in England as well as in Scotland. As earl of Huntingdon, David was lord of a greater part of the English East Midlands. The Garioch, his main holding in Scotland, covered about 260sq km (100sq miles) between the outskirts of Aberdeen in the south-east and Strathbogie (now Huntly) in the north-west. He had other estates, including those in and around Dundee, but his life was largely spent at his two chief castles, at Fotheringhay (Northamptonshire) and Inverurie. Today, Fotheringhay is much better known in connection with another Scottish royal, Mary Queen of Scots, who was executed there in 1587.

The contrast between the impressive Bass of Inverurie and the humble motte castle at Balmaclellan, in Kirkcudbrightshire, could not be greater. The latter is quite small (**7**), standing 6m (20ft) high with a summit measuring just 10m (33ft) in diameter, and there is no trace of an accompanying bailey. It is hard to see the motte alone serving all the needs of its lord, and we must assume that some form of outer enclosure existed, though not necessarily one raised above the ground. At Southwick

Motte, in eastern Kirkcudbrightshire, aerial photography hints at an enclosed but unelevated area beside the motte itself, and at the Motte of Montfode, close to Ardrossan (Ayrshire), excavation revealed the existence of two outer ditches which, although of unknown date, may conceivably have been part of the bailey defence.

We know neither when Balmaclellan was built nor by whom. We assume a twelfth- or early thirteenth-century date, though the lesson of Roberton (Lanarkshire) serves to caution us about making such statements in the absence of excavation (see page 56). The builder of Balmaclellan could either have been an incomer or a native Gallovidian. Either way, it is reasonable to assume from the physical remains found at Bamaclellan that its owner was not in the same league as Earl David of Huntingdon.

One puzzle about these Scottish mottes is their distribution throughout the country. Although there are examples in east-central Scotland, in the Lothians, in Fife and north of the River Tay, the vast majority are clustered in areas which in the twelfth and early thirteenth centuries were on the periphery of the realm and which posed real problems for the monarchy, regions like Galloway and Moray. The obvious conclusion to be drawn is that motte castles were more likely to be built in districts where political unrest was a distinct possibility. This was after all how the motte castle probably originated, as a quick and comparatively cheap solution to providing a lord with the necessary security against attack. It has been estimated that an average-sized motte, 5m (16ft) high and 15m (50ft) across at the top, would have taken fifty people about forty working days (assuming a ten-hour day) to construct. All they needed were their muscles, their digging tools and a good site foreman; only the joinery work required specialist skills.

7 Balmaclellan Motte, Kirkcudbrightshire, on the skyline to the right of the parish kirk, is fairly typical of Scottish mottes – small, lacking a bailey, and about which scarcely anything is known.

There were certainly forms of castle other than mottes in Scotland, and contrary to modern perception, the motte was probably the exception rather than the rule. After all, much of the country was relatively peaceful and the incoming lords managed, by and large, to settle their new estates without much difficulty. Take Freskin, for example, a Fleming who came to Scotland late in King David's reign. He clearly felt insecure in his estate in Moray as his mighty motte-and-bailey castle at Duffus, near Elgin, demonstrates; the rebellion of the men of Moray, ruthlessly put down by King David in 1130, must have been a factor in Freskin's decision to build in such a formidable manner. But before moving north to Moray, Freskin was already settled in Lothian, as lord of Strathbrock, near Livingston. Today there is no trace of his lowland castle, and although it is just possible that it may have been a motte castle which has not survived, it is far more likely that it was something less robustly built but just as serviceable as his lordly residence. So what were the alternatives open to Freskin?

We know both from documentary evidence and through fieldwork that islands, whether in rivers or lochs, were used for lordly residences. Uchtred of Galloway was murdered at his island fastness in the River Dee, possibly Threave, in 1174. The landscape of medieval Scotland for the most part was altogether boggier than it appears today and there was thus a greater opportunity to exploit the terrain to this

8 A typical Scottish crannog, on Loch Earn, in Perthshire. On nearby Loch Tay, a modern crannog has been constructed, based on recent archaeological excavations in the loch, giving a fascinating insight into how these watery residences might have looked.

end. Islands had an innate defensive quality requiring little more than an encircling wall of wood or stone to make them reasonably secure. They might be natural islands or man-made constructions called crannogs (**8**). One of the two crannogs in Lochrutton Loch (Kirkcudbrightshire) has been recently dated by dendrochronology to the late twelfth or thirteenth century.

Perhaps the most common form of castle, though, was the one where the castle area remained on the same level as the surrounding ground but which was defended by a raised earthen bank fronted by a ditch. Archaeologists call them 'ringworks'. They were not as defensively strong as mottes, nor as impressive in the landscape, but they would nevertheless have been perfectly adequate and acceptable fortified residences in the more peaceful areas of the country. But ringworks, being less robust than mottes, have probably been easier for farmers to remove over the past two centuries. As a consequence they are now few in number. Perhaps a good proportion of those cropmark sites recently discovered through aerial photography, and prosaically termed 'miscellaneous' for the want of a more precise categorization, may turn out on excavation to be ringwork castles.

A fine example of a ringwork castle is that built for Robert Croc at Crookston ('Croc's toun'). Referred to about 1180 as his 'close' or court, a date confirmed by pottery found during excavation in the 1970s, it consists of a single ditch encircling a large area crowning the summit of a low hill (see **4**). We know nothing of the nature of any buildings that might have stood therein, although a chapel is mentioned in the records. One thing is certain; the views from the top of Robert's residence would have been as outstanding then as they are today from the summit of the late-medieval tower house.

The surviving physical evidence for these early castles is almost entirely confined to their defences. The buildings themselves are now all gone, with three notable exceptions.

The tiny stone-built chapel of St Margaret in Edinburgh Castle was built during the reign of King David; it was much altered in later centuries before being restored by the Victorians. It is an odd building in several respects, and recent speculation has raised the intriguing possibility that it was not intended as a free-standing building but as part of a larger, secular structure, perhaps a tower-keep like that at Bamburgh (Northumberland). Given King David's close personal relationship with Henry I of England, his building such keeps is perfectly plausible. Indeed, there is proof that he did so, and this is the second of our exceptions.

The imposing keep in Carlisle Castle (Cumberland) was built in the second quarter of the twelfth century, most probably by David following his capture of the fortress in 1135, although a recent reassessment hints at the possibility that the foundations may have been laid by Henry I in the late 1120s. Notwithstanding, David of Scotland was certainly instrumental in its construction, and such was his attachment to the building that it became his favoured residence. He even kept his will there. Appropriately, it was in the little chapel on the second floor of the keep that he passed away on 24 May 1153. Yet within four years of his death the castle was back in English hands and his 'grand tur' came to be enjoyed by Henry II.

9 An impression of how Aberdour Castle, Fife, might have looked in 1200 (Harry Bland).

The third exception is now lost amid the clutter of later medieval stone buildings at Aberdour Castle (Fife). It is the stump of a stone keep, measuring some 16 by 11m (52 by 36ft) over walls almost 2m (6ft) thick, whose construction may be dated to the late twelfth century from the evidence of the double-lancet window, the cubical masonry, the flat, clasping buttress at the north-east corner and the splayed base course. The surviving fragment (the structure was later heightened and greatly remodelled throughout) suggests a free-standing building perhaps two or three storeys high, probably comprising a hall on the first floor above an unvaulted basement (**9**). The lord of Aberdour at this date was William de Mortimer, a friend of Earl David of Huntingdon and the Garioch, and it may have been he who built this remarkable survival from a bygone age. William may also have been responsible for the building of the church a little to the south-east of the castle, one of the best preserved Romanesque churches in Scotland.

The physical nature of castles – the excavated evidence

Only through excavation are we able now to discover more about these early castles, about the nature of their defences and of the buildings themselves, and from the associated artefacts form some impression of everyday life in the castle. Unfortunately, despite our long interest in, and fascination with, castles, very little archaeological investigation has been carried out, with the result that our understanding is still very limited. Of these excavations some, like those at the Mote of Urr (Kirkcudbrightshire), Duffus and Crookston, have done little more than provide a twelfth-century date of construction for the original earthworks. Others, including those at Castlehill of Strachan, the Peel Ring of Lumphanan (both Aberdeenshire) and Roberton, have demonstrated that the motte castles there were not built until the later thirteenth century at the earliest (see pages 43 and 56).

The excavations have on the whole been more successful in throwing light on the nature of the defences than in illuminating the domestic arrangements. The picture painted by Guillaume of powerful strongholds defended by ditches or moats is borne out by the spade. Neither Ralph Rufus's motte at Barton Hill (Perthshire) nor that at Rattray (Aberdeenshire) had an encircling defence visible before excavation but both in the event revealed impressive ditches, 2m (6ft) deep, which had subsequently been abandoned and filled in. The castle of the bishops of Glasgow, sited immediately to the west of their great cathedral, was entirely lost from sight until recent excavations uncovered evidence for a large ringwork 28m (92ft) in diameter enclosed by a deep ditch. Atop the motte at Auldhill, Portencross (Ayrshire), a stronghold of the de Ros family, were found the foundations of the gatehouse entrance comprising three opposing sets of twinned post-pits; we can picture the heavy oak doors creaking back and forth. From Portencross, Rattray and Barton Hill has come evidence for a perimeter defence around the edge of the motte. At

10 The summit of the motte at Barton Hill, near Kinnaird, Perthshire, during excavations in 1972. Ranging poles indicate the four massive post-pits supporting the timber tower. A stretch of the stone-revetted encircling wall is visible in the background.

Portencross this took the form of a palisade of large timber posts, but at Rattray the summit was enclosed by a slight rampart revetted with clay and stone which may have had a timber palisade behind it. At Barton Hill the rectangular enclosure was defined by a drystone wall base that supported either a turf bank or a timber palisade (**10**).

Evidence for the buildings themselves has come from several castle sites. At Barton Hill and Keir Knowe of Drum (Stirlingshire) the evidence was relatively unambiguous, for each was found to have a square structure, probably a tower or keep, at the centre of the motte summit but nothing else. Both towers measured 5sq m (54sq ft)

on plan. A small rectangular building was also found in the west half of the royal castle at Peebles, which may have been some form of service building. Beside it, though, was a larger circular structure. A similar sub-circular building was revealed in the northern part of Rattray motte. These twelfth-century sub-circular buildings (another smaller example has been found at Cullykhan, Banffshire) defy interpretation; were they roofed towers or enclosures open to the elements?

But it is from Cruggleton that the most revealing evidence for castle buildings has come. We have already encountered this impressive castle through the pen of Guillaume le Clerc (see page 15), whose portrait of Soumillet's 'handsome home beside the sea' captures perfectly this stronghold hugging a rocky clifftop overlooking Wigtown Bay (see **5**). The rebuilding of the castle's defences in stone in the later thirteenth century resulted in the destruction of the earlier defences – Guillaume's 'clay and wattle walls' – but the excavations carried out in the late 1970s showed that the present motte was created in the later twelfth century, around the time of Roland, by extending a natural rocky outcrop at the cliff edge out to the north and west. This created a summit area about 30m (98ft) across and standing some 4m (13ft) above the expansive bailey on the landward side. Dominating the motte summit was a complex timber building interpreted as a long ground-floor hall, measuring 12.5 by 4m (41 by 13ft), with a tall tower, 4m (13ft) square, attached to it at the north-west corner. Perhaps this was the very 'tower that was not made of granite or limestone with ramparts and battlements' from which Soumillet 'could see for thirty leagues all round'.

The Norse legacy

The name Soumillet is a corruption of Somerled (*sumarlidi*), Norse for 'summer raider'. This reminds us that in the twelfth century the writ of the king of Scots did not extend as far as it did in King James III's reign in the mid-fifteenth century, when Scotland reached its present extent with the acquisition of the Northern Isles, *Orkneyjar*, from Norway and the final loss of Berwick-upon-Tweed to England. Not only the Northern Isles but Caithness, and much of the Outer and Inner Hebrides off Scotland's west coast (*Sudreyjar*) lay beyond the control of King David and his successors. Nominally this huge area was under the sovereignty of the kings of Norway (**11**). In reality, Orkney, Shetland and Caithness were ruled by Norse earls governing almost independently of the Norwegian monarchy, while much of the western seaboard was ruled by a Gaelic aristocracy infused with Norse blood, among whom Somerled, lord of Argyll, and his sons were pre-eminent. We shall encounter the sons of Somerled in the next chapter, for the thirteenth century was their great castle-building age. But from the Northern Isles and Caithness comes evidence of castle building in the time of King David.

The evidence is both literary and physical. The *Orkneyinga Saga*, written down about AD 1220, vividly recounts the story of the jarls and odallers who inhabited this northern archipelago a thousand years ago. The saga writer portrays a hectic life of summer raiding and winter fuelling, of warring and wassailing. It is a bloodcurdlingly good read. If ever a society needed castles for its protection, this was it. Yet the impression we get from reading the *Saga* is of residences which were for the most part unfortified farmsteads, with a large feasting-hall at their centre. The seat of Earl Paul in Jorfiara (Orphir, in Orkney) in 1136 seems typical: a large homestead standing on a hillside with an impressive drinking-hall next to the church. Recent excavations there have uncovered beside the upstanding ruin of the church the remains of a large building that may be the 'drinking hall' referred to. The saga evidence for undefended homesteads is corroborated by archaeological evidence at sites such as Jarlshof, at the southern tip of Shetland, where at no point in the period of Norse occupation from the ninth through to the thirteenth century is there any hint of fortification.

Where strongholds are specifically referred to they are described either as borgs or castles, but the distinction, if any, is not readily apparent. It may be that the saga writer meant 'borg' to imply a stronghold of some antiquity and 'castle' a new type of defensive building. Certainly 'Moseyjarborg', the borg in Hjaltland (Shetland) where Erlend Ungi 'made great preparations for defence' against Earl Harald Maddadson in 1155, is the well-known Mousa Broch built about 1,000 years earlier. A borg in Caithness, Lambaborg, seems also to be a place of last resort, a retreat for Swein and his companions from the murdering Margad. It is described as 'a strong place . . . situated on a sea-girt rock, and on the landward side there was a well-built stone wall', which conjures up a picture of a late prehistoric promontory fort rather than a medieval castle.

By contrast, the references to castles imply new structures. Four castles in the region are specifically referred to in the *Saga* – one on the island of Damsay, another on Wyre, a third in Kirkwall, and the fourth at Thurso in Caithness. It is the castle on Wyre that is of the greatest interest because the saga writer's description is complemented by the physical remains of the castle itself.

11 Yet another raiding party of Vikings from Norway prepares to disembark from its fleet of longships. The Norsemen first descended on northern and western Scotland around AD 800, and subsequent kings of Norway ruled in the West until 1266, and in the north until 1468–9.

Of Cubbie Roo and other towers

Cubbie Roo's Castle stands on a ridge at the north end of the island of Wyre. Close by is the ruined twelfth-century St Mary's Church, and the modern farm name, the Bu of Wyre, recalls the great Norse drinking-hall that would have preceded the stone castle as the family residence, and possibly continued in use alongside the new castle. The saga writer tells us that about the year 1150 Kolbein Hruga, the young man who lived in the island, 'built a fine stone castle, which was a strong defence'. Kubbie was a Norse nickname for Kolbein; hence the corruption of his name to Cubbie Roo.

Kolbein Hruga's castle consisted of a small stone tower, 7m (23ft) square, over walls almost 2m (6ft) thick. All that exists today is the lower part of the basement storey. There is no ground-floor entrance and a ladder from above must have reached this cellar. The only features are two slit windows and a water tank sunk into the ground. The original height of the tower is impossible to determine, but three storeys

*12 How Cubbie Roo's
Castle, on Wyre,
Orkney, might have
looked in 1231, when
Earl John Haraldson's
assassins sought refuge
there and held out
against the earl's
avenging friends. On the
right is the little late
twelfth-century church,
and in the background
the Bu of Wyre, with its
great feasting hall
(David Simon).*

would have given reasonably clear views across Gairsay Sound (**12**). The outer defences around the tower were subsequently abandoned and built over. However, excavation has shown that the original fortified area, measuring 29 by 23m (95 by 75ft), was protected by a 2m (6ft) deep flat-bottomed ditch with a stout stone wall on the inner lip and a low earthen rampart along the counterscarp.

The building of castles by the Norsemen may at first sight seem surprising. Although they came from the same root as the Normans, by the twelfth century their social and political culture was very different from that of their southern kinsmen. But this is to ignore the remarkable degree of contact between the men from the north and the rest of the known world. Two examples will suffice to illustrate this. King Sigurd Magnusson, who succeeded to the throne of Norway in 1103 following his father's death in Ireland, set out on a pilgrimage to Jerusalem in 1107 which took him the best part of three years to accomplish; his people gave him his by-name 'the Jorsala-farer' on his return. And the *Orkneyinga Saga* recounts in fascinating detail Earl Rognvald's three-year voyage on crusade to the Holy Land in the 1150s. Such voyages must inevitably have brought the Norsemen into contact with the new-fangled castles;

indeed, the saga writer regales us with Rognvald's successful attack on a castle in Galicialand (Galicia in north-west Spain). The confrontation has everything: missiles raining down on both camps, boiling pitch and brimstone being poured from the battlements, and the piles of burning faggots melting the lime holding the castle walls together – all great stuff! Such encounters must have made an impression on the Norsemen. In the unsettled, blood-spattered society of the Northern Isles so excitingly depicted by the saga writer, there was surely a place for the castle.

The Norsemen's encounters with castles were not always hostile for there was peaceful contact with other nations, including Scotland. This included marriage alliances. Harald Maddadson, earl of Orkney from 1139 to 1206, for example, had an Orcadian mother but his father was Matad, earl of Atholl. And when Harald himself married in about 1150, he took as his lady Affrica, daughter of Earl Duncan of Fife, the builder of Cupar Castle. It seems likely that Earl Harald was the builder of castles. The stone towers, or keeps, at Braal, near Thurso, and Old Wick (both Caithness) have both been credited to him. The latter lies on a narrow spine of rock projecting into the North Sea a little distance south of Wick town (see page 2). The upstanding tower at the neck of the promontory has marked similarities with Cubbie Roo, like the lack of a ground-floor entrance and the narrow slit window lighting the basement. But the ruined shell of Old Wick rises much higher than Cubbie Roo, giving us further clues as to its appearance. It was entered at first-floor level and was entirely unvaulted throughout its four storeys, its wooden floors resting on ledges around the walls. The fireplaces did not have flues rising through the thickness of the walls but clay smoke-hoods attached to the inside faces. There is no evidence for either mural stairs or wall chambers, but the loss of most of one wall prevents us from saying whether such ever existed. Beyond the tower and spread out over the rest of the promontory are the foundations of stone buildings that presumably complemented the lord's accommodation within the keep.

The stone towers at Cubbie Roo, Braal and Old Wick stand in marked contrast to the contemporary castles built within the realm of Scotland, where the prevailing impression is one of earth and timber. But the abundance in Orkney and Caithness of good building stone for the mason, and the dearth of trees for the carpenter-joiner, must be chiefly responsible for this difference. Earl Harald's brother-in-law, Earl Duncan II of Fife, also built a great castle on his lordship of Strathbogie (subsequently renamed Huntly) in Aberdeenshire towards the end of the century. It was a motte-and-bailey castle in the Norman tradition (see **77**). But given the evidence we have from the *Roman de Fergus*, and from the excavations at Barton Hill, Cruggleton and elsewhere, who is to deny that, other than the choice of building materials, Earl Duncan's timber tower atop his motte at the Peel of Strathbogie was any different in form and function than Earl Harald's stone keep at Old Wick, or Kolbein Hruga's on Wyre.

2

A golden age of castles:
the thirteenth century

Now they [the Norwegians] collected their force and their ships, about the islands; and they got eighty ships. And they sailed south round the Mull of Kintyre, and so in to Bute. The Scots sat there in the castle; and a certain steward was over the Scots. They proceeded to the castle, and made a hard assault on it, but the Scots defended themselves well, and they poured down upon them boiling pitch and lead. The Norwegians bound over themselves shields of wood, and they hewed the wall, because the stone was soft; and the wall fell down after that. The torchbearer, who was called Skagi, shot the steward to death at the moment when he leapt upon the castle wall. They fought with the castle men for three days, before they won it. There they took much treasure, and one Scottish knight, who ransomed himself for 300 merks of refined silver.

When the west was won

The dramatic story of the Norwegian assault on the castle of the Steward of Scotland at Rothesay in 1230, related in *Eirspennill's Hakon Hakon's son's Saga*, is the earliest account we have of an assault on any Scottish castle. The action marked the beginning of the end for any claim to suzerainty the kings of Norway had over the *Sudreyjar*, the western seaboard of Scotland, for although the northmen were successful in taking the castle on this occasion, they were compelled to withdraw shortly afterwards. When King Hakon IV returned with an even bigger force thirty-three years later, and once again besieged and took the castle, he met with misfortune off the Ayrshire coast near Largs and withdrew to Kirkwall where, in the hall of the bishop's residence, he died two months later. The Treaty of Perth, signed by Hakon's successor, King Magnus, and the king of Scots, Alexander III, in 1266 effectively brought the lands and islands of the west under Scottish control. Scotland was about to enter a 'golden age'. It was certainly a golden age as far as castle building in Scotland was concerned.

The besiegers of Rothesay Castle in 1230 were, in fact, headed not by a Norwegian but by Gillespec (Uspak in Norse) MacDougall, a grandson of Somerled. Somerled had spent a lifetime amassing a great lordship stretching from Gigha in the south to the Uists in the north, playing one realm off against the other as well as beating off the predatory activities of the kings of Man, masters in the Outer Hebrides and quite possibly Skye too. Somerled's descendants, including the MacDougalls and the MacDonalds, built on that success. But they were not the only players in the field, for other families of Celtic stock made the most of the situation, like the MacSweens, the MacLachlans and the Lamonts. All were fiercely independent and proud of their roots, and they have given us a lasting treasure, one of the most

marvellous collections of stone castles anywhere (**13**).

The rugged coastline of Argyllshire and western Inverness-shire is dotted about with castles. The vast majority belong to a later era. However, among them is a group whose origins lie in this period when the west was won for Scotland. The history of fortification in the region, of course, reaches back much further, into the Iron Age. The fact that many of the later castle sites have the prefix *dun*, generally meaning 'fortified hill' but which in this part of the country could equally describe a prehistoric broch or dun, suggests a continuity of fortified settlement of which the medieval castle was the last in the sequence. Archaeological excavation has shown how Iron-Age duns, like that at Dun Lagaigdh beside Loch Broom in Wester Ross, continued as fortified residences long into the Middle Ages.

We now have no way of knowing just who the people were who lived in Dun Lagaigdh in the Middle Ages, or quite what their status in society was, although the discovery of a large coin hoard secreted there around 1230 suggests they were people of substance. Perhaps another site in the region holds a clue. Dun Ringill, hugging the cliff-edge overlooking Loch Slapin in the south-east of the Island of Skye, is so evidently a structure of Iron-Age date – a near-circular, thick-walled drystone structure with one very narrow entrance passage complete with door-checks and bar-holes, and one intra-mural cell (**14**). However, two features betray the fact that this ancient fortress was still serving as a stronghold (a *borg* in the jargon of the saga writers) in the medieval period: a ditch around the outside and the foundations of two rectangular buildings within. Although Dun Ringill has a shadowy history, it is reputed to have been the traditional seat of the MacKinnon chiefs before they moved to Caisteal Maol at Kyleakin ('Hakon's Narrows'; King Hakon sailed through here in 1263 on his way to the battle of Largs). Dun Ringill may well then be typical of the fortified residences of many of those holding maritime lordships across the western seaboard in the thirteenth century. There were others, though, who were moved to build afresh in an alien tradition.

13 A depiction of a castle, possibly Dunvegan on Skye, on the tomb of Alasdair Crotach MacLeod, lord of Dunvegan (died 1547), in St Clement's Church, Rodel, Harris.

14 Dun Ringill, beside Loch Slapin, on Skye, an Iron-Age defensive structure refortified and reoccupied in the Middle Ages, probably by the clan chief of the MacKinnons.

Castle Sween and the new curtain-walled castles

These new castles characteristically have high walls; we call them curtain walls. They enclosed areas of ground irregular in shape but normally rectilinear and not circular on plan. They are all in their own way impressive structures, but Castle Sween, crouched on a rocky ridge beside Loch Sween, is arguably the most awesome of all (**15**). It is also one of the few we can date reasonably closely by its architecture, for the quadrangular enclosure has shallow pilaster angle buttresses at the four corners, similar to what we saw at Aberdour. Such clasping buttresses are indicative of a late-twelfth century date, in which case Sween was built by Suibhne (Sven) 'the Red', a man with both Gaelic and Norse blood coursing through his veins. Sween and Aberdour together are thus the oldest datable standing castles in Scotland. Confidence in this remarkably early date is further underpinned at Sween by the simple, round-headed entrance gateway through the south wall, similarly contained within a pilaster buttress.

There is nothing quite like Castle Sween anywhere else on the western seaboard, and Castle Tioram, in Loch Moidart, is more truly representative of the group (**16**). It stands proudly on top of a rocky promontory that is cut off from the shore at high tide. The enclosing curtain wall is over 2m (6ft) thick and rises to an average height of 10m (33ft) (but to twice that along the seaward side). A towering height and a massive thickness are characteristics of the curtain-walled stone castles of the thirteenth century. The height gave an immediate advantage to the defenders in this pre-gunpowder age; the thickness not only made life more difficult for the miner but also gave sufficient width to support a wall-walk on the battlements.

The curtain wall is almost entirely featureless – there are no windows or slits – and only the two entrances (one, the old postern, now blocked) and the embattled parapet relieve the grey severity of the curtain. The tall tower house that rises above the wall in the north-west corner was clearly added at a much later date and there is

15 Castle Sween, Argyllshire, with Jura and Mull in the distance. The residence built by Suibhne, progenitor of the MacSween family, in the late twelfth century, is now the oldest standing castle in Scotland.

now no evidence of the form the original residential buildings took. But Tioram retains much of its original defensive arrangements. These include a small stone box-machicolation supported on stone corbels above the main entrance from where one of the defending garrison could 'cover' the vulnerable gateway beneath (there are traces of another over the postern); a stone stair hugging the inside face of the wall giving access to the battlements; and the embattled wall-head itself, with its wall-walk protected on both sides by parapet walls, and clear signs in the put-log holes on the outer face and the scarcements along the inner face that the wall-walk was originally protected by timber hoards.

Castle Tioram was the principal stronghold of the chief of Clan MacRuari, descended from Somerled. Other 'sons of Somerled' have left a similar legacy, including the MacDougalls at Dunollie and Dunstaffnage, both close to Oban, and the MacDonalds at Mingary, in Ardnamurchan. Similar castles in the group include Duart on Mull, Duntrune beside Loch Creran, and Dunvegan on Skye. The marked similarity of these castles begs the question of whether a single hand was involved in their design and execution. Of all these, only Dunstaffnage has round towers projecting from the curtain wall and openings through it, in the form of 'fish-tail' arrow-slits and lancet windows (**17**). Recent excavations have shown that the main north tower was an early addition to the curtain wall; in which case all three towers, and possibly also all the openings through the curtain wall, may not be original.

The arrow-slits and windows at Dunstaffnage are among the few architectural details throughout the entire group which are reasonably closely dated – to some time in the thirteenth century. The owners of Dunstaffnage during this time are also well documented, making their castle an important guide to the rationale behind the building of these alien constructions.

16 Castle Tioram, Loch Moidart, Argyllshire. The lofty, thick curtain wall was largely defended from the battlements, either from the little box machicolation sticking out over the entrance gate (on the right) or from projecting timber hoards (now gone) supported on timbers placed in the putlog holes (visible near the wall-top).

17 How the MacDougalls' residence at Dunstaffnage, beside the Firth of Lorn, Argyllshire, might have looked about 1275. The projecting round towers may have been early additions to the original rectangular enclosure wall. The MacDougall lordship was essentially a maritime one, hence the galley-house for the lord's own galley, and the fleet out in the firth. (David Simon).

At the time of the Norwegian attack on Rothesay in 1230, Sir Duncan MacDougall, a grandson of Somerled, was lord of Lorn, an extensive maritime lordship; in fact, it was Duncan and his two brothers, Gillespec and Dugald, who led the assault against the Stewarts' Bute stronghold. Contrary to what one might believe, Duncan and his peers were no 'small-time' petty chiefs operating on the very fringe of the known world; they were major landholders, had large forces and fleets at their disposal, and wielded significant political clout. Duncan moved easily between the two realms that competed for his loyalty, and journeyed widely, including to Rome as an ambassador of the king of Scots in 1237. His travelling clearly broadened his mind for in about 1230 he established at Ardchattan, beside Loch Etive, a priory for Valliscaulian monks from Burgundy. In the light of this, his building of a formidable castle in the European tradition need come as no surprise.

Duncan's son, Ewen, who inherited the lordship in the 1240s, followed in the same mould. Initially throwing in his lot with King Hakon, he succeeded in becoming 'king' over all the Isles, from Man to Lewis. However, by the time of Hakon's expedition in 1263, Ewen had transferred his allegiance back to the king of Scots, which in the short term led to his imprisonment but which turned out to be a shrewd move in view of what then happened to the Norsemen. Ewen MacDougall of Lorn now became pre-eminent in the region, the Scottish king's chief representative in Kintyre, Argyll and Lorn. We can see this reinforced power and prestige being reflected in a flurry of building activity. It is tempting to ascribe to him the projecting round towers and the great hall along the east side of the enclosure at Dunstaffnage, which together furnished the lord with much improved private and public accommodation.

Hall castles

Formidable enclosures were not the only form of castle introduced into the west at this period. At Aros on Mull, Carrick on Loch Goil, and Skipness in Kintyre are rare examples of hall castles. There were doubtless more, but being less substantial structures they have not survived so well the rigours of time. Recent excavations at the Campbell stronghold of Carrick may provide the first archaeological dating for the construction of these somewhat unusual structures, the architectural dating of which has hitherto ranged across the spectrum from the late thirteenth to the late fourteenth centuries. If the Saintonge ware found in the primary levels relates to the construction of the present impressive structure, then a date in the closing years of the thirteenth century seems the most likely.

Skipness Castle provides a good example of just how vulnerable these hall castles were to change. The present stronghold looks for all the world like a mighty enclosure castle dating from the close of the thirteenth century, but embedded in the fabric are substantial remains of an earlier hall castle. This comprised two freestanding buildings, one of them a two-storey residence, with the lord's hall on the upper floor – hence the generic name – and the other floor containing a single-storey chapel. There may well have been other structures as well, and everything would probably have been enclosed within a defensive wall of earth and timber. The MacSweens held Skipness around the middle of the century, and it is possible that this more modest castle was a subsidiary residence to their main house beside Loch Sween.

All these strongholds, whether curtain-walled castles or hall castles, were built primarily as residences for their lords. But there is clear evidence that they were built very much with royal approval, and with the distinct possibility that the monarchs themselves might desire to use them on those occasions when they were in the region. Alexander III's charter to Gilchrist MacNachtan, lord of Fraoch Eilean ('Heather Island') Castle in Loch Awe, empowers him 'to have the custody of our castle and island of Frechelan, so that they may cause the said castle to be built at our expense, and to repair it whenever necessary, and to keep it in safety for our needs, and to make the said castle, honourably prepared, open for us to dwell in on such occasions when we may come there'.

These castles of the western seaboard are quite extraordinary strongholds. Here in Argyll and the Isles, far beyond the Norman pale, rose some of the most impressive castles built in the thirteenth century, rivalling anything being constructed in the realm of Scotland itself. Yet Suibhne and his peers were not feudal aristocrats of Norman stock but chiefs with mixed Norse-Gaelic roots. What possessed them to build as they did will forever remain a mystery, but our legacy of castles is the greater for their efforts.

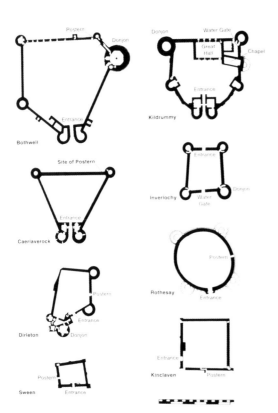

18 *Some thirteenth-century curtain-walled castle plans compared.*

Mainland castles of the great and grand

The winning of the west for Scotland was achieved in large part through the endeavours of the Stewarts. It was Walter, first of the hereditary Stewarts, who very probably defeated and killed Somerled himself in battle near Renfrew in 1164; and it was his son, Alan, who made the first inroads into the western sea when he took control of the Island of Bute some time before 1200. Sixty years later, Walter Stewart, earl of Menteith (see **23**), contrived to oust Dugald MacSween, son of Suibhne 'the Red', from the lordship of Knapdale.

The Stewarts, unlike the MacSweens, were fully paid-up members of the Anglo-Norman aristocracy and the building of high and mighty stone castles, to replace their more modest timber strongholds of the previous century, would for them have been the perfectly natural thing to do. In this they were mirroring the activities of their close relatives in England, in particular the FitzAlan lords of Oswestry, the descendants of Walter (I)'s eldest brother, who during the course of the twelfth century built impressive masonry castles at Arundel (Sussex) and Clun (Shropshire), on top of or, in the case of Clun, into the original earthworks. Given the close family ties binding the Stewarts despite their residing in different countries, and given also the fact that the Scottish Stewarts retained certain English estates inherited from Walter (I), we can picture Walter's descendants becoming familiar with these and other English castles as they travelled south to visit relatives and friends and administer their lands. In this the Stewarts were far from alone, and we should never underestimate the amount of travelling undertaken by the Scottish aristocracy in those far-off days of the twelfth and thirteenth centuries, and particularly the extent of their contacts with their English peers.

Nothing survives above ground of Renfrew Castle, the Stewarts' chief residence, which is a great pity for it must have been something to marvel at if what we have left at their two other principal seats, Dundonald and Rothesay, is anything to go by. Dundonald has only recently been excavated to reveal more of the sophisticated castle built on that prominent hilltop towards the close of the century. Rothesay on the other hand stands remarkably intact (**19**), albeit somewhat altered down the centuries, and although its original date of construction is not possible to determine it was most probably built either by Alan, who died in 1204, or his son, Walter (II). Rothesay and Sween are thus contemporary.

Despite the obvious difference in their shapes – Rothesay circular and Sween rectangular – the two castles in their original states were much alike. Rothesay shared the same solidly thick stone curtain wall – a well-nigh impregnable shell (though they reckoned without the Norsemen and their axes!) within which were placed the main castle buildings, now all gone. The main entrance was a single timber door set behind plain stone jambs terminating at the top in a round arch and secured by a draw-bar; the postern was similar. There were no other openings through the curtain wall, except perhaps for the crenellations at the wall-head, reached from the courtyard by two flights of stairs.

The strong curtain wall with the emphasis on wall-head defence was the chief characteristic of the great thirteenth-century castle. Typical is Kinclaven Castle, close to the confluence of the rivers Isla and Tay north of Perth. It survives only as an ivy-clad ruin and has never been excavated, but we know that it was built by the crown between 1210 and 1236 following the destruction in a great flood of the royal castle at Perth. The square curtain wall encloses a substantial area 40m (131ft) across that would once have been crammed with buildings (see **18**). A modest amount of accommodation would also have been provided in the small towers projecting from the curtain, one at each corner, and although little remains of these they may have

19 *Rothesay Castle, the Stewart stronghold on Bute. The original circular curtain wall, built about 1200, was furnished with projecting round towers, a battered wall base and crenellations in the later thirteenth century. King James IV added the imposing gatehouse on the left about 1500.*

20 Dirleton Castle, East Lothian. The cluster of projecting round and rectangular towers (left foreground) provided private accommodation for Lord and Lady de Vaux.

been similar to the latrine tower projecting from one of Sween's corners. Similar rectangular towers projected out from the curtain wall at another imposing early thirteenth-century castle, Balvenie, near Dufftown (Banffshire), built most probably by William Comyn, earl of Buchan, who died in 1233. Also visible at Balvenie, but gone from Kinclaven, is a stretch of wall-walk on the battlements of the curtain. Gone from Balvenie but existing at Kinclaven is the straight stone stair giving access to the wall-walk.

Two significant developments affected these simple curtain-walled castles as the century progressed. One was the addition of large round towers to the angles of the curtain, and the other was the strengthening of the entrance defences. Both seem to have been prompted chiefly by a need to upgrade security, but the towers also contributed to important improvements in the accommodation.

Projecting round towers first made their appearance in castles around 1200; Chateau Gaillard, the extraordinary castle overlooking the River Seine, in northern France, may well have been a major influence in their gradual spread in the early years of the century. The earliest instance in Scotland that can be dated with a degree of confidence to the second quarter of the century is Dirleton Castle, in East Lothian, built by John de Vaux (**20** and see **18**). Though the de Vauxs had close family links with England – John's cousin, Robert, was lord of Gilsland in Cumbria – it seems more likely that the inspiration for the multi-towered Dirleton Castle was drawn from France. John de Vaux became steward to Queen Marie de Coucy following her marriage to King Alexander II in 1239. Marie was the daughter of Duke Enguerrand (III), lord of Coucy, near Amiens. Enguerrand's castle, built in the 1220s, was largely destroyed by German troops during World War I, but we are fortunate in that MacGibbon and Ross recorded it a generation earlier. They showed it to be a mighty polygonal curtain-walled enclosure with four formidable round towers projecting from the angles and a massive round tower, or donjon, housing the lordly accommodation, dominating all. John de Vaux must surely have visited Coucy while accompanying his queen on her visits home; he can have been nothing but overwhelmed by what he saw.

John de Vaux's motive for building such a formidable residence must surely have been his earnest desire to display wealth and status. He was after all no marcher lord but a landed nobleman holding a comparatively small but exceptionally rich barony in the heart of the kingdom – a kingdom largely at peace with itself, and with its southern neighbour, thanks to the Treaty of York signed in 1237. The only conflict of any substance was taking place in the Norse dominions many miles to the west.

Herein lies one of the contradictions of the medieval castle. It originated in the tenth and eleventh centuries in times of strife to help protect and defend, but such times were not conducive to the building of large, imposing and costly residences. For Lord de Vaux to build a great stone castle he needed three things: he had to have the wealth to build it; he had to have reliable tenure of his lands; and he had to have lengthy periods of peace to carry out the building works, which would have taken many years to complete.

Caerlaverock – a tale of two castles

The development of the curtain-walled castle from the relatively simple rectangular form to the more complex round-towered type is well illustrated at Caerlaverock (**21**), situated at the mouth of the Nith estuary in Dumfriesshire. Caerlaverock has not one but two castles and, as luck would have it, the construction date for both was accurately established in the 1970s by dendrochronology. The older castle in the woods was shown to have been built in the mid-1220s, shortly after Sir John de Maccuswell (Maxwell) was granted the barony. Sir John chose to transfer his chief seat from his ancestral estate near Roxburgh Castle in the eastern Borders (see **33**) to his new lordship. This site has recently been excavated and found to be quadrangular in plan with three small rectangular towers added to the curtain, in the manner of Kinclaven Castle.

The Caerlaverock Castle that so impresses visitors today was built 200m (218 yards) to the north of the original castle about 1277, the date the drawbridge timbers were felled (**21** and **22**). The Maxwell lord at this date was Herbert, Sir John's nephew, but his reasons for going to such time, trouble and expense after barely fifty years can only be guessed at; the most convincing explanation is that the first castle had been built too near the salt-marsh of the Solway Firth and become unstable. The 'mark II' castle was quite different from its predecessor. The writer of the splendid poem, the *Roll of Karlaverock*, composed in celebration of King Edward of England's great siege of the castle in 1300, described it perfectly: 'In shape it was like a shield, for it had but three sides round it, with a tower at each corner, but one of them was a double one,

21 Caerlaverock Castle, beside the Solway estuary, Dumfriesshire. Although much of the upstanding masonry belongs to the fourteenth century and later, the unique triangular plan dates from the time of the castle's foundation in the 1270s.

22 The drawbridge timbers discovered in 1962 during excavation of the inner moat at Caerlaverock Castle. Dendrochronological dating showed that the original bridge had been built in the 1270s, that it had been repaired in the 1330s, and completely replaced by a new bridge in the 1370s – dates that mirror the fortunes of Scotland before, during and after the wars with England.

so high, so long, and so wide, that the gate was underneath it, well made and strong, with a drawbridge and a sufficiency of other defences' (see **18**).

Other members of the 'great and grand' were moved to build in a manner similar to Herbert de Maxwell, and examples may be seen throughout the country. Caerlaverock was unique in being triangular; the others were more conventionally shaped. Even here there was variety, particularly regarding the location of the principal lordly accommodation. Some, like Caerlaverock, had the twin-towered gatehouse serving as the keep, where the lordly accommodation was housed; these have been christened 'keep-gatehouses'. The royal castle at Kirkcudbright seems to have been of this form, and the Stewart stronghold at Dundonald also. In fact, recent excavation has shown that Dundonald had two imposing gatehouses, similar to the Edwardian castles at Rhuddlan and Beaumaris in Wales. One gatehouse faced eastward into Scotland and the other westward to the Stewarts' newly acquired island dominions beyond the Firth of Clyde.

The majority of castles, however, had the lord's residence housed in a mighty tower, or donjon (the word has subsequently been corrupted into 'dungeon', with an altogether different meaning), placed elsewhere along the curtain wall's circuit. John Comyn's formidable stronghold at Inverlochy near Fort William (Inverness-shire) is the perfect illustration of this. There the rectangular curtain wall has four round towers, one at each corner (see **18**). Three are identical but that at the north-west corner is 3m (10ft) bigger in girth. The castle built most probably by the earl of Mar at Kildrummy in Strathdon (Aberdeenshire) has a polygonal-shaped curtain wall with several round towers projecting from it. However, that at the west corner, the Snow Tower, is over 4m (13ft) larger than the Warden Tower at the north corner (see **18**). Kildrummy also has a twin-towered gatehouse, sadly now surviving as foundation walls only, but there is good reason for thinking that this element was grafted onto the curtain wall during the English occupation of the early 1300s.

There is no getting away from the fact that each castle was different from the next, despite the common use of the basic ingredients – high curtain wall and projecting round towers. Various arguments have been advanced as to why, for example, some castles had the lord's residence over the gatehouse and others had it housed in a donjon elsewhere in the enclosure. As far as I am aware no one has advanced the possibility that the difference was the result of personal preference, of 'one man's meat being another man's poison'. Many things may have changed down the intervening centuries, but one thing is for sure, human nature has not; and man's penchant for doing the unpredictable was probably just as true then as it is today.

The baronial household

To understand better how the baronial castle functioned as a residence we have to know something of the structure of a great nobleman's household. Unfortunately there are few surviving documents that give us an insight into the workings of a Scottish baronial family, and we have to complement what we have with those relating to baronial families in England. This seems reasonable enough, for several Scottish noble families held estates south of the Border. However, we must exercise caution when doing so; in 1295 the annual income of the earl of Fife was assessed at £500 thus placing the leading earl of the Scottish realm on a financial par with a modest English baron. The exercise, however, is worthwhile for it enables us to peep into their world, a world so different from our own.

The baronial household was varied in composition and large in size. In fact, there was probably more than one household, for the lady of the castle would have had a household, and an independence, of her own. Lord and lady lived largely separate lives, he forever travelling about, visiting his various estates, attending on his king and so forth, she residing more permanently at the castle, seeing to the running of the place and the upbringing of the family (**23**). The children in their early years stayed in the castle, though they were largely brought up by nurses who were expected to feed, wash, teach and comfort them. It was usual for children from about the age of five, girls as well as boys, to be sent away to another noble household to further their education. They would return in their early teens to take their place in the bosom of the family once more. Girls were normally married by the age of 14, whereas boys generally waited until they had come of age and into possession of land in their own right.

Life in the castle was male-dominated; women had a very low profile. Other than her ladyship herself, her ladies-in-waiting, the nurses and perhaps the laundress, almost everyone else was male, though oddly enough the beer was often produced by an alewife! Given the large numbers in the household and the cramped nature of the accommodation, perhaps this largely all-male world was just as well. The household comprised men from all levels of society. There was the body of knights, squires and men-at-arms who provided the lord with his quota of military service (**24**); the small nucleus of senior officials who managed his affairs; the larger group of lesser office-bearers who carried through the wide range of functions required to sustain the lifestyle of a great nobleman; and the vast underbelly of 'gofers'. All told there may have been as many as 150 people living and working in and around a great castle.

At the top of the tree was the steward. It was his duty to supervise the managing of the estates and the running of the household. There might in fact be two stewards,

23 Countess Mary of Menteith clasps Walter Stewart, her husband, affectionately to her bosom on their double effigy, now on display in the chapter house at Inchmahome Priory, on the Lake of Menteith, Stirlingshire. The loving couple, who together accompanied the maid Margaret, daughter of King Alexander III, to Norway in 1282 for her marriage to King Eric II, were buried side by side in the choir of the priory church.

24 *The effigy of an armed knight of the Stewart earls of Menteith, on display in the chapter house at Inchmahome Priory.*

for by the mid-thirteenth century it was becoming common practice to separate out estate management from household management. The estate steward would have been a man of noble birth in his own right, not far removed in rank from the lord himself and very probably residing on his own manor, where he too would have been served by his own more modest household. The household steward on the other hand is more likely to have been of less noble birth and to have lived more permanently at his lord's castle in his own quarters. To him fell the task of ensuring the smooth running of a busy and varied complex that was expected to function as family home, soldiers' barracks, guest house, estate office, law court and prison.

Other officials assisted the steward. These included the constable, responsible for security, the chamberlain or treasurer, in charge of the finances, and the pantler and butler, who together looked after the provision of food and drink. The chaplain, who also acted as the lord's secretary, administered the spiritual side of things. The almoner salved the lord's conscience by attending to the poor at the gate. Beyond the immediate confines of the courtyard were the marshal, who had charge of the many horses and the baggage-train which transported the lord and lady and their travelling household around the country.

Each official had charge of a host of assistants, lower-ranking servants and menials who actually carried out the work. Under the constable were the porters, who guarded the castle gates, and the door-wards or ushers, who watched the doors leading into the great hall and the private apartments of the lord and lady. Several clerks assisted the chaplain, including the clerk of the writing office and the clerk of the chapel, who in turn supervised others, including the sacristan and the choirboys. In the kitchens, working to the direction of the pantler and butler, was a proliferation of cooks, larderers, saucers, pantrymen, bakers, brewsters and poulterers. Elsewhere there was the tailor, the barber-surgeon who let blood and drew teeth as well as shaved his betters, and the chandler who ensured that folk didn't fall down the winding stairs in the dark. Beyond the courtyard, under the watchful eye of the marshal, were the sumpters, farriers, grooms, carters and messengers who went hither and yon about the realm with dispatches. Of course, not every baronial household would have been so extensive; everything was relative. But somebody of the highest rank and station, like Walter of Moray, lord of Bothwell, might well have commanded something approaching the complement given above.

Bothwell and the castle as residence

Bothwell, built beside a winding in the River Clyde 12km (7½ miles) south-east of the centre of Glasgow, is without any doubt the most imposing of all the great thirteenth-century castles, then as today (**25**). Not for nothing has it been called 'the grandest piece of secular architecture that the Middle Ages have bequeathed to us in Scotland'. In common with its contemporaries, Bothwell has suffered down the

25 Bothwell Castle, Lanarkshire, and the River Clyde.

centuries, but despite the various prolonged and bloody medieval sieges and the undermining by coal miners of more recent times, the walls still stand today, monumentally impressive. It is the perfect castle to illustrate how life was lived in these mighty fortress-residences. And there was no one greater or grander than Walter of Moray, who acquired the lordship of Bothwell in 1242 on the death of his father-in-law, Walter Olifard II, and who very probably began the building of the mighty castle. In fact, so grand were the Morays that Walter's son and heir, William, who succeeded him in 1278, was known as 'the Rich'.

With the picture of a great baronial household in our minds, the enormous scale of Bothwell Castle begins to make sense (see **18**). It matters not one jot that the original scheme for a huge polygonal-shaped courtyard covering 0.75 hectares (1.8 acres) (putting it on a par with mighty Caernarfon) never reached fruition – perhaps William 'the Rich' became 'the Poor' as his money ran out, or maybe the wars with England after 1296 intervened – for it does not in any way detract from the intended magnitude of his castle or deflect from our appreciation of the enormous size of his household. If in our mind's eye we people the now quiet and ghostly ruined castle with a great household such as I have described, we can perhaps begin to imagine what life

26 How the mighty castle of the Morays at Bothwell might have looked in 1275 had the original building programme been completed. On the far bank of the Clyde is Blantyre Priory, a small Augustinian house founded around the 1240s by the earl of Dunbar (David Simon).

in a great thirteenth-century castle would have been like (**26**). Just imagine the stench from the cess-pits at the bases of the latrine chutes! No wonder they chose to move about from place to place at frequent intervals, giving a chance for the steward to arrange for a good clean-out.

Bothwell's mighty curtain had five round towers projecting from it. One of them was a twin-towered gatehouse that most likely provided quite commodious living quarters in its upper floors for the constable and his personal servants. Three of the other four towers would also have provided apartments for other senior officials on their upper floors, each perhaps comprising two rooms – a hall on the first floor and a private chamber containing the bed on the second, directly beneath the battlements. The rooms would have had fireplaces and latrines *en suite*. The personal servants might have slept on 'shake-downs' laid out either on the floor of the bedchamber or in the passage outside the door.

The ground floors of all the towers were given over to stores, whether for arms and ammunition, for food and drink, or for other miscellaneous items. The smallest of the towers 'stored' prisoners in both its ground floor and basement. Imprisonment was not a form of punishment in the Middle Ages, not formally anyway, though it seems that many an unfortunate was thrown into prison and suitably forgotten about. Poor Sir Patrick Lindsay, for example, was cast into a dark dungeon in Rothesay Castle in 1489 and told to 'sitt quhair he should not sie his feet for ane year'. Prisons like that at Bothwell were more commonly used to hold suspected criminals until they could be brought for trial in the baron court where, if they were found guilty, they would be sentenced to other forms of punishment, like paying a fine or losing a hand. The two-tier prison at Bothwell – the prison and pit – is a good example of many a castle prison in Scotland. The upper level is reasonably well ventilated and lit by the narrow arrow-slits and has a latrine; the miserable pit beneath lacks sanitation, light or air. We assume that the prison itself was for the freemen in society and the pit for the serf class. Those of noble birth would normally have been held under permanent guard in one of the officials' apartments.

The largest of the towers, the mighty donjon, was the residence of the lord and his immediate family (**27**). Even today in its ruined state it impresses, just as it was intended to overawe those who gazed on it all those years ago. Everything about it proclaims that therein resided a man of immense power and wealth. The red sandstone masonry is of the highest quality ashlars, the architectural detail is restrained but refined, and the planning is so carefully and cunningly thought out that it provided both a spacious and a secure suite of rooms. The accommodation was spread over four floors: a storage basement complete with well, a ground-floor reception hall, and two upper floors that together formed the lordly apartment.

Despite the fact that one half of 'that stalwart toure' has now gone, cast down in 1337 by its owner, Sir Andrew Moray, in order to prevent the castle from being garrisoned again by the English, the remainder stands largely complete from basement to wall-head. The huge courtyard on the other hand is now devoid of its clutter of buildings. Pride of place would have been the hall block, probably a two-storey timber structure, located near the donjon for the lord's convenience. The great hall itself on the upper floor was the setting for all the great occasions – large feasts, gatherings of the household and tenants, sittings of the baron court. Below it, at ground level, there may have been a 'laigh' or lower hall, or perhaps storage space. The kitchens, bakehouses and stores would have stood close by. Elsewhere there would have been brewhouses, stables, workshops, even perhaps

27 The donjon of the Morays at Bothwell, built in the later thirteenth century but partially destroyed during the Wars of Independence, is recognized as the finest piece of medieval secular architecture surviving in Scotland.

a little castle garden for the lord and lady's use and a kitchen garden growing vegetables and herbs. Beyond the curtain wall would have been orchards, dovecots and rabbit warrens, and beyond them still the 'park' where the lord would spend many a happy hour hunting and hawking.

Lesser castles

The castles referred to above were without exception the chief residences of the élite in society, the royal family and the leading magnates. But below them were castles of lesser magnitude. These served a variety of functions. Some were subsidiary residences of the great and grand, perhaps located on an outlying estate, serving as a hunting-lodge or possibly protecting a feature of strategic importance such as a harbour or river crossing. Others were the permanent residences of the lesser nobility. These might be knights holding their lands as sub-tenancies of the main fief; they might be noblemen serving as high-ranking officials in a mighty lord's retinue, like that of estate steward; or they might be barons of second rank holding their lands as individual fiefs directly of the crown. As might be expected, these lesser castles were less impressive structures than the likes of Bothwell. Most of them were the timber castles constructed in the previous century, while those built during the course of the thirteenth century continued to use the readily available raw materials of earth, clay and wood in preference to the more costly stone and lime.

28 The Peel Ring of Lumphanan, Aberdeenshire (centre foreground), with the Grampian Mountains in the distance. That such apparently 'minor' castles could serve the 'high and mighty' just as well as great stone strongholds is further borne out by the fact that Edward I of England, 'Hammer of the Scots', spent a night there in August 1296, during his 'whistle-stop' invasion of Scotland.

Lumphanan – a hunting-lodge

Hunting was an important leisure pursuit of the medieval nobility and most great castles would have had forests or deer parks associated with them. Considerable time was spent away from the main residence by the great and grand looking for sport, and so hunting-lodges were common. These were generally defensive in form, such as Alexander II's hunting-castle at Clunie, in the southern foothills of the Grampians.

Excavations at the Peel Ring of Lumphanan, Aberdeenshire, in the late 1970s demonstrated beyond doubt that the motte had been built around 1250, and not as had previously been thought a century earlier as part of the 'Normanization' of the province of Mar (**28**). The lord of Lumphanan by this date was Sir Alan Durward, who not only laid claim to the earldom of Mar, but was also earl of Atholl and holder of extensive estates north of the Firth of Tay as well as at Bolsover in the English Midlands. Sir Alan must only have been able to visit Mar infrequently, where hunting was probably the chief attraction. He and his hunting party would ride out from Coull Castle, his chief residence just 4km (2 miles) from Lumphanan, and spend several days and nights in the 'forest', using Lumphanan as their hunt-hall. At another Aberdeenshire motte, Castlehill of Strachan, 15km (9 miles) from Lumphanan, recent excavations have shown that this too had been built as a hunting lodge, for the de Giffards of East Lothian. It is tempting to see the several oven bases found outside the hunt-hall as medieval barbecues, around which the party gathered at the end of a day's sport, eating and drinking and regaling each other with tales that were as long as the night.

Muirhouselaw – a moated manor

The permanent residences of those on the next rungs down the social ladder, the knights and the lairds, seem generally to have taken a similar form to the lesser castles of the élite in society. Mottes, ringworks, islands and crannogs constructed by forebears in the preceding century also continued to be occupied.

However, a new form of fortified home – the moated homestead or manor – probably made its appearance in Scotland during the century, although there has been an almost complete absence of excavation to verify this. It seems reasonable to assume that the development mirrored that south of the Border where much more work has been done. The picture emerging there is of moated sites originating in the latter half of the twelfth century and proliferating during the course of the next two centuries.

Moated sites come in all shapes and sizes. Hallyards (Perthshire), known only from aerial photographs, measures 85 by 80m (279 by 262ft), whereas that at nearby Links is a mere 30m (98ft) square. The laird of Hallyards is not known. However, if size is anything to go by, he must have been higher up the social ladder than the probable builder of Links, William, son of Alexander, a tenant of Richard de Montfiquet, lord of the barony of Cargill, where there is a fine ringwork. Moats could be quite complex in form. The site at Gelston (Kirkcudbrightshire), now also largely visible only from the air, has two adjacent moated enclosures, one perhaps serving as an outer court to the main residence, in much the same way as the bailey served the motte. That at nearby Dunrod was demonstrably an integral part of a developed community, with a church and village close by.

Muirhouselaw Moat (Roxburghshire) is a fine example. It comprises two contiguous enclosures of unequal size, the larger measuring 70sq m (753sq ft), and the smaller about half that size. Both were surrounded by a broad, flat-bottomed ditch, evidently intended to be filled with water. Within the larger enclosure are the stone foundations of two structures, the larger one a two-roomed building measuring about 20 by 9m (66 by 30ft) and the smaller one 5sq m (54sq ft). We can postulate that the former was the hall block for more public activities, and the latter a square tower housing the lord's private apartment, much like the arrangement at Cruggleton. Less substantial buildings, housing the kitchen, storage cellars, a chapel, a stable and the like, probably stood close by. The smaller enclosure may have served as a garden.

Muirhouselaw may be equated with the 'Morhus' mentioned in the Melrose cartulary and held by the de Normanvilles in the thirteenth century. Lest such residences of earth and timber be regarded as in some way inferior in status to those built of stone and lime, one event in the history of Muirhouselaw speaks volumes. In 1379, negotiations between Scottish and English commissioners for a peace between the two countries, as well as a marriage between Richard II of England and a daughter of Robert II, were conducted there.

Rait – a hall castle

Rait Castle (Nairnshire) is a rare survival of a hall castle, a building that must have been far more common across the country than is generally supposed (**29**). Earlier in the chapter we saw similar hall castles scattered about the western seaboard, such as Skipness whose very existence remained undetected until earlier this century. Further examples, including Lochranza (Arran) and Craigie (Ayrshire), have similarly become cloaked in later castle guises, begging the question just how many more await discovery. Others may have been completely demolished when the time came to build afresh, or allowed to fall into ruin when the site was abandoned. Future excavations will undoubtedly find more examples. The supposedly seventh-century monastery building near St Abb's Head (Berwickshire) turned out on investigation in 1980 to be a later medieval secular hall.

Rait, like Skipness, is a two-storey building, measuring about 20 by 10m (66 by 33ft), with an unvaulted basement and an upper hall. The hall was entered directly from the outside through an impressive doorway protected by a portcullis and a drawbar. There would have been a screen closing off this end from the hall itself and forming a lobby; it may have had a minstrels' gallery above it. At the far end of the hall from the screen would have been the high table, the 'hie burde', where the lord and his family took their meals, bathed in sunlight streaming through the large windows confined to this end of the hall, and heated by the handsome hooded fireplace. A projecting round tower, entered from the 'hie burde' end, housed the lord's private apartment and a narrow rectangular projection on the other side of the building was the latrine. The basement, unheated and indifferently lit, was probably used for storage. There seems also to have been an attic in the roof space, from which access was gained to a defensive wall-walk. The kitchen and other service rooms were probably housed in timber buildings in the barmkin or courtyard outside; the remnant of one such structure is visible attached to the gable beside the doorway. All were enclosed within a perimeter wall.

The manor of Rait first appears on record in 1238, but on architectural grounds the hall castle must be dated to the end of the century, in which case it may have been built by either Sir Gervaise de Rait or his younger brother, Sir Andrew. We know very little about either of them. Gervaise was appointed constable of the royal castle at Nairn during the interregnum following the untimely death of Queen Margaret 'the Maid of Norway' in 1290, and both men were certainly caught up in the stirring events that followed the invasion by King Edward I of England six years later.

29 The entrance front of Rait Castle, Nairnshire. The two pointed windows beyond the first-floor doorway lit the lord's hall, while the projecting tower at the far end housed the lord's private apartment.

3

The wars with England: the fourteenth century

But notwithstanding such assaults made upon them, those within did not surrender, but so defended themselves that they held out, in despite of all, all that day and night, and the next day till terce. But greatly their courage and force Brother Robert depressed during the attack, who sent there many a stone by the robinet, from dawn to night the day before he had not ceased. Moreover on the other side he was erecting three other engines, much larger. And he bends and bends again, puts stones in the sling, discharges and splits everything he hits. Nothing resists his blows, bretasche nor great timber. Yet they did not flinch, but held upon their defence, those within, until the roof fell in on all sides, whereby the stones entered; And whomever one of them struck, neither iron cap, nor wooden target, saved him from being wounded.

Castles under attack

The years of peace and prosperity that had characterized King Alexander III's reign were brought to a sudden and horrible end on Friday 30 March 1296. On that fateful day King Edward I of England with his 30,000-strong army crossed the River Tweed, stormed the walls of Berwick, then Scotland's chief burgh and port, and ran amok through the streets; by Sunday most of the male inhabitants had been butchered. This appalling atrocity heralded fifty years of bitter conflict, and thereafter continuing mistrust and periodic warfare, between the two countries. The thirteenth and fourteenth centuries have with justification been described as a hundred years of peace occasionally interrupted by war, followed by a hundred years of war occasionally broken by peace – a century of 'jaw-jaw' followed by a century of 'war-war.'

If Scotland's great thirteenth-century castles had been built to defend, then now was the time to prove themselves. In fact, almost without exception they were found sadly wanting. Berwick Castle fell along with the town. Less than a month later, following the defeat of the Scottish host at Dunbar on 27 April, the garrisons of the other principal royal castles – Roxburgh, Jedburgh, Dunbar, Edinburgh, Stirling, Lanark and Dumbarton – surrendered their charges without a fight. Mighty Edinburgh, atop its invincible volcanic plug (see **1**), where the State records and crown jewels were kept, withstood three days and nights of murderous artillery bombardment before it was given up. In stark contrast, by the time the English reached equally impressive Stirling, they found only a humble gatekeeper waiting for them with the keys!

This picture of formidable stone strongholds being yielded by their garrisons with barely a fight is repeated throughout the wars with England, the so-called 'wars of independence'. And the English experienced just as much difficulty hanging on to their prizes as the Scots.

Stirling's story is typical. Following its capture by the English in 1296, Stirling remained under their control until its recapture in September of the following year following William Wallace's audacious victory at Stirling Bridge. The castle was as long in Scottish hands when it was wrested back by the English in July 1298 following Wallace's defeat at Falkirk. The Scots retook the stronghold late in 1299, and this time they managed to cling on to it until another mighty siege by Edward of England in July 1304 forced them out once more. King Robert Bruce's great victory at nearby Bannockburn in June 1314 saw the castle return once more under Scottish control. But this time, rather than attempt to hang on to it, Bruce ordered the destruction of its defences so that the fortress could not be held against him again. And so matters rested until the outbreak of war again following Bruce's death in 1329 and the accession of his five-year-old son, David. By 1336 Stirling was in English hands once more, and in the following year they managed to fend off a Scottish siege. They were not so fortunate in the winter of 1341–2 and were eventually starved into surrendering. Stirling would not fall into English hands again until Cromwell's successful siege in 1651.

It was not only the royal castles but also the great baronial castles that were put to the test; and they fared no better. Not even formidable Bothwell Castle could withstand siege. In 1298–9 the English garrison contrived to hold out for fourteen long months. Stephen de Brampton, the English commander, in a report to his king, told of how he had defended the castle 'against the power of Scotland for a year and nine weeks, to his great loss and misfortune, as all his companions died in the castle except himself and those with him who were not taken by famine and by assault'. Two years later the English retook it in less than a month.

There were notable exceptions to this undignified failure of the castle to withstand attack. One of the most renowned was Black Agnes's defence of Dunbar Castle in 1338. (Agnes Randolph, countess of Dunbar, was called black 'be ressone scho was blak skynnit'.) So stoutly did her garrison resist that it brought the English king, Edward III, to the castle in person to review the proceedings. In vain he watched his navy, his war engines, his sappers, his engineers and crossbowmen attempt to wrest the fortress from Black Agnes's grasp, the whiles having to endure the humiliating spectacle of the formidable lady standing on the castle battlements hurling abuse as well as missiles at the besiegers. Six months and £6,000 later, King Edward beat a tactical retreat.

With the benefit of hindsight, the disastrous turn of events after 1296 might be seen as justification for the building of Scotland's great thirteenth-century castles. But those who built them were not to know that relations with England would deteriorate so rapidly after the death of Alexander III. Quite the opposite, in fact, and so shaken were their descendants by the way things had turned out that they looked back to Alexander's reign with nostalgia and christened it a 'golden age'. That most of Scotland's castles were found wanting when put to the test suggests either that the architects who designed them had got it badly wrong, or that defence against a fully-pressed siege was not the primary concern of the builder. The latter explanation seems the more plausible.

Castles were built primarily as centres of lordship, outward and visible statements of the power and authority of those holding land and controlling everything and anything that dwelt on it. Their main purpose was to furnish their lords with the multi-functional accommodation they needed to enable them to carry out their political, legal and social duties. This involved providing a measure of protection for the lord's family, household and retinue against a variety of threats – thieves and robbers, hostile neighbours, civil disorder and foreign aggression – the idea being to make life as difficult as possible for as long as possible for those determined to break in uninvited. But no fortress was impregnable.

Siege warfare

There are a number of accounts of sieges during the wars, and these give us an inkling as to how Scottish castles were attacked and defended. During Edward I's summer campaign of 1301 a field army of 6,800 men, including 20 masons and 20 miners, laid siege to Bothwell Castle (**30**). The turning point of the siege was the arrival before the castle of a giant siege engine called 'le berefrey' (belfry), a lofty wooden tower on wheels or rollers, several stages high, and with a drawbridge at the top that could be dropped onto the battlements of the castle. It had been prefabricated in Glasgow and trundled the few miles south to Bothwell. A bridge had to be specially built over the Clyde to aid its progress, and a corduroy road laid up to the castle so that the awesome machine could be wheeled against its walls. The English Wardrobe

30 An impression of Bothwell Castle under siege by the English in 1301. The outcome turned on the arrival at the scene of a mighty siege tower called 'le berefrey' (belfry). Built in Glasgow at great expense, it required 30 wagons to transport it to the castle. The ten-mile journey took two days (David Simon).

Accounts that furnish us with this information do not inform us as to what happened next. However, the great machine must have played a significant part in the outcome of the siege, for within the month it was making its way to the siege of Stirling Castle, its work at Bothwell satisfactorily completed.

Stirling itself endured a particularly bitter siege in the late spring and early summer of 1304. By then it was clear to Edward I of England that his subjugation of Scotland would not be achieved until he retook Stirling. During the winter of 1303 Edward, safe within his headquarters at Dunfermline Abbey, finalized his siege plan. He would take no chances; a formidable array of siege engines, seventeen at least, was to be deployed. So proud were the English of their artillery that they had pet names for them. One was called 'Bothwell', presumably 'le berefrey' that had been at the siege of Bothwell three years earlier. Another had the terrifying name of 'war wolf'. Quite what 'war wolf' did is not made clear, but it may have been a trebuchet, a mighty stone-throwing machine, for when it was fired at the castle it devastated the gatehouse. In truth, the English king had no need to deploy 'war wolf' at all for the garrison had previously surrendered, so depriving Edward of the thrill of seeing his latest 'toy' in action for the first time. Not to be denied his moment of pleasure, he ungraciously ordered part of the Scots' garrison back into the castle so that he might show off his new weapon.

War engines clearly played an important role in siege warfare, as the illustration on the charter granted in 1316 to the city of Carlisle for resisting the Scots in the previous year so tellingly shows (**31**), but they were only part of the story. The 20 miners at the siege of Bothwell were there presumably to attempt to cut their way either through or under the castle walls, much like the Norse had done at Rothesay in 1230, their purpose being to cause a collapse so that the awaiting infantry might rush through the breach and take on the defenders in hand-to-hand fighting. These

31 Scottish artillery at the siege of Carlisle, 1315, illustrated in Edward II of England's charter to his Border city, granted in the following year.

aggressive acts were supported by more passive tactics, the 'waiting game', by which the castle was blockaded and the defenders prevented from gaining fresh supplies. Many a siege was allowed to drag on in the knowledge that eventually those within the castle would be reduced to starvation, as Stephen de Brampton experienced at Bothwell. For this reason, garrisons, knowing they were about to be besieged, took the precaution of stocking up in advance. Unfortunately, this worked against the unlucky garrison defending Kildrummy in the summer of 1306; they were compelled to surrender to the English when the fire that began in the great hall, where extra grain had temporarily been stored, quickly got out of control and spread throughout the rest of the castle.

The siege of Caerlaverock, 1300

32 Edward I of England's siege of Caerlaverock, 1300, drawn by David Simon. Full details of the two-day siege of Lord Maxwell's stronghold beside the Solway Firth were recorded in a contemporary account, the Roll of Karlaverock.

The progress of the majority of the sieges may only be glimpsed at in contemporary records, mainly financial accounts and monastic annals. But there was one siege, the English investment of Caerlaverock Castle in July 1300, for which we have full details (**32**). The *Roll of Karlaverock*, a snippet from which introduced this chapter, is a remarkable poem for it gives us a blow-by-blow account, literally, of the action by someone who was actually there. The author was an unnamed herald serving in Edward of England's army as it set out from Carlisle on 1 July to invade Galloway. No matter that the poet's prime purpose in penning it was to record the heraldry of the English knights-in-arms, nor that his language is dripping with hyperbole for dramatic effect; it nevertheless remains a wonderful word-picture of the whole process of besieging a castle.

The English force that arrived before Caerlaverock on that day in July numbered 87 knights and 3,000 infantry. The castle garrison ranged against them, we subsequently discover, comprised just 60 men and the lady of the castle, Lady Maxwell; her husband was by then languishing in an English prison. Our poet, though, was under no illusion as to the enormity of the task confronting his side:

> Caerlaverock was a castle
> So strong, that it did not fear siege,
> Before the king came there;

He offered his opinion:

> It will not be taken by check with a rook,
> But there will be projectiles thrown,
> And engines raised and poised.

The besiegers first pitched camp, under the direction of the marshals:

> There was many a cord stretched,
> Many a peg driven into the ground,

after which they helped the navy to unload the engines and provisions that had newly arrived by sea. The siege could now begin in earnest. The first assault was made by the infantry, who took the full brunt of the garrison's opening salvo:

> And might be seen fly among them
> Stones, arrows, and quarrels [crossbow bolts].

The men-at-arms rushed forward in support, but they too came under heavy fire from the defenders stationed at the battlements:

> Stones fall so thickly,
> As if they would rain them,
> And hats and helmets crushed,
> Shields and targets broken in pieces;

Defiantly they returned fire, picking up the fallen stones and hurling them back at the defenders, thereby contriving to reach the brink of the ditch. There, one of their number, Thomas de Richmond, stepped boldly forward onto the bridge and shouted out to the defenders demanding entry. The response was predictable, and the stones rained down once more. But still they pressed the attack, with Adam de la Forde mining at the walls and Richard de Kirkbride assailing the castle gate:

> For never did smith with hammer

Strike his iron so hard
As he and his did there.

All to no avail. The huge stones that were showered down on them, along with the arrows and quarrels, eventually forced them to retire. Further waves of attack were likewise repulsed:

Those within, who are fully expecting it,
And bend their bows and cross-bows,
And shoot with their springalds [a mechanical cross-bow],
And keep themselves equally ready
Both to throw and to hurl.

Throughout all this, Brother Robert (a holy man of God!) kept up a constant barrage from his stone-throwing 'robinet'. But realizing this to be inadequate, he ordered his men to build three much larger engines. The resultant effect was devastating, as the quotation at the beginning of this chapter details. First, the bretasche, or timber hoard protecting the wall-walk, was hit, and one of the defenders sheltering behind it killed. Then the roof behind collapsed under the weight of the hurled stones. The defenders now had no option but to surrender, and so, after little more than a day of stout resistance, they did so:

The companions begged for peace,
And put out a pennon.

The author of the *Roll of Karlaverock* leaves us with the firm impression that much of the defence was carried out from the wall-head. This involved men armed not only with longbows and crossbows but also with stones, and very probably anything else that came to hand. Many a castle still has its share of crude sandstone balls lying around, none more so than Caerlaverock itself, while excavation at others has produced plenty of arrowheads and crossbow bolts. A good cross-range was retrieved from Urquhart Castle (Inverness-shire) during clearance work in the 1920s, including clumps of corroded arrowheads, evidently once stored in a bag long since rotted away.

The archers on the battlements were assisted by others firing small mechanical engines – springalds, firing much larger crossbow bolts, and stone-throwing catapults. Elsewhere in the castle others would be attempting to beat off the assaults. Some would be stationed within the projecting towers, firing their arrows and bolts through the narrow slits at the miners hacking at the bases of the walls or at those attempting to batter down the castle gate. The experiences gained and the lessons learned during the course of these 'wars of independence' would lead to improvements being made to castle design. Wall-heads, gateways and outer defences in particular were prime features for recrafting.

English strongholds on Scottish soil

The prolonged attempt by the English to impose themselves on the Scots resulted not only in them using Scottish castles as bases from which to operate but also in them building new strongholds. Unfortunately, despite there being considerable documentary evidence in the English accounts for the repair and rebuilding of captured Scottish castles, little physical evidence survives on the ground. There are just two significant survivals, in addition to the fragments of masonry lurking behind the ivy atop the mighty castle hill of Roxburgh (**33**). One is at Kildrummy in the north of the country and belongs to the heady days of the first 'war of Independence'; the other is Lochmaben (Dumfriesshire) near the Border and dates to the twilight of the English occupation in the 1360s.

The ruined gatehouse at Kildrummy is so similar to that at Harlech Castle, in north Wales, that its construction has been attributed to King Edward I's mason-architect, Master James of St George, who was responsible for building Harlech in the 1280s. Edward twice stayed at Kildrummy, in 1296 and 1303. Shortly after the latter occasion, Master James received £100 for work undertaken. The records are not specific, and the work for which he was reimbursed may not even have been carried out at Kildrummy, but the timing and the similarity with Harlech suggest otherwise. The sum involved was large for those days and compares with the £125 paid by Edward for the building of another great north-Welsh castle gatehouse, Conwy.

Master James was one of a number of skilled contractors, if we may call them that, brought to Scotland from Wales after 1296. They included Master Walter of Hereford, master mason at Caernarfon, and Thomas de Houghton, a master carpenter fresh from Beaumaris. Not only were they engaged in repairing and rebuilding captured castles, they were also practically involved in the sieges themselves, constructing siege works and engines. However, their most important contributions have now all but vanished – the stronghold built by Master James at Linlithgow (during 1302–3) and other strongholds at Lochmaben and Selkirk. These new works were known as 'peels', from the Old French word *pel*, meaning stake, for they were built almost entirely of wood.

The peel at Linlithgow (West Lothian) was built around the royal manor house erected during King David I's reign in the twelfth century, on the site where the palace

33 Roxburgh Castle (centre foreground), strategically sited between the rivers Tweed (left) and Teviot (right). The burgh of Kelso lies in the distance. The fragments of masonry on the summit of the mighty castle hill are a legacy of the lengthy English occupation. The remains of the town of Roxburgh, which at one time was second only to Berwick-upon-Tweed in importance, but withered as the English presence in the Scottish east march continued, lie beneath the green sward beyond the castle. The last siege of Roxburgh Castle, in 1460, finally ended the English occupation.

of the later Stewarts now stands (**34**). The main element was a great ditch cutting the promontory off from the town to its south, behind which was the peel or palisade, made of split tree trunks. In the centre of the palisade was a strong gatehouse, which possibly incorporated some stonework, and at either end, beside the loch, were wooden towers. A lesser ditch and a palisade were constructed around the remainder of the promontory to defend it from attack from the loch. Inside the peel, fresh garrison buildings were erected to complement the old manor house.

Despite being built largely of earth and timber, Linlithgow Peel stood the test better than most masonry castles and stayed in English hands until after Bannockburn in 1314. Even then it was only taken by a cunning ruse when a local man, William Bunnock, hid eight armed men in his hay-cart and halted it right in the middle of the gateway to prevent the portcullis from being lowered. The peel survived until 1424 when a great fire swept through the town and destroyed both it and the ancient royal seat.

The second significant survival is Lochmaben Castle, Dumfriesshire. We know that the English built a peel there in 1298, which changed hands several times before being taken back by the English in 1333. The strength then remained in enemy hands until Archibald 'the Grim', scourge of the English, finally retook it for Scotland in 1385, the last English outpost other than Roxburgh remaining on Scottish soil. It was during these last decades of English occupation that major works were carried out at the garrison, as the excavations undertaken there in the 1970s confirmed. The works included the refortification of the old peel, possibly so that it could be used as a protected work camp for the stonemasons, carpenters and others labouring on the imposing stone castle rising up behind.

There may have been another type of English stronghold built in Scotland but which has to date escaped detection – temporary camps for the king and his retinue while on campaign. As Edward I led his field army about the country he normally availed himself of captured castles and compliant monasteries for his temporary quarters; that is how he came to be at Kildrummy and Dunfermline. But there may well

34 Linlithgow Loch from the east. The English peel was built on the promontory jutting into the loch from the left-hand side, where the later palace and parish church now stand.

have been occasions when this proved impracticable. After capturing Caerlaverock in July 1300, Edward continued on his invasion of Galloway and remained for a short while at Girthon, west of Kirkcudbright. But where precisely? Was it the motte castle now in the woods behind Cally House, or could the nearby earthwork (now intriguingly known as 'Palace Yard') have been built specifically for his use? It is a simple enough site, an oval area of ground enclosed by a bank and ditch; the bank was presumably palisaded.

Temporary residences

Bruce's policy of rendering captured castles incapable of further use certainly made life more difficult for the English in the shorter term, but where were those lords whose castles had been 'razed to the ground' expected to reside thereafter? Such was the predicament faced in 1337 by Sir Andrew Moray of Bothwell, the grand-nephew of William 'the Rich', when, having just wrested his ancestral castle back from the enemy, he yielded to the patriotic necessity of pulling down one half of his mighty donjon (see **25**). The short answer is that we have no real idea. Some castles may have been repaired. Tree-ring dating of the bridge timbers at Caerlaverock (see **22**) has shown that the original bridge of the 1270s was patched up in the 1330s, but this coincides with Edward Balliol's arrival on the scene and with Sir Eustace Maxwell of Caerlaverock's change of allegiance (yet again) – he repaired and garrisoned the castle before placing it at Balliol's disposal. And so the question still remains: where had Sir Eustace and his household been living for the preceding twenty years, since 1312 in fact, when he had received financial reward from Robert Bruce 'for demolishing the castle'?

It is just possible that the nobility abandoned their great stone castles while hostilities lasted and withdrew to less substantial residences of earth and timber. These are likely to have taken the form of moated manors, which were reasonably cheap and quick to construct but which offered a measure of defence against limited attack. The internal buildings would not have been anywhere near as grand as those they had recently abandoned, but this was war – and in war, anything goes.

That such residences were perfectly acceptable to the senior nobility is demonstrated by the action of King Robert Bruce himself. In 1326 the ageing monarch acquired an estate at Cardross, on the opposite bank of the River Leven to the royal castle of Dumbarton. There he had a manor house built which became his home in the autumn of his days. It contained a hall, chambers for him and Queen Elizabeth, a chapel, kitchen and larder. We read in the records of plastered and painted walls, glazed windows and thatched roofs. Beyond the confines of the house there was a garden, and a park where the king indulged his passion for hunting and falconry. It was at Cardross that he died three years later.

The motte castle seems also to have made a comeback during this troubled time. It was, after all, conditions such as the Scots were now experiencing that had created the motte in the first place. Like the moated manor, it was quick and inexpensive to construct, but its extra height improved its defensive capability. Unexpected confirmation that mottes were still being constructed in Scotland in the early

35 Roberton Motte, near Biggar, Lanarkshire, under excavation in 1978. Pottery from the old ground surface beneath the motte dated its construction to no earlier than 1300.

fourteenth century came in the 1970s during excavation of a motte near Roberton in Upper Clydesdale (**35**). Pottery found beneath the mound unequivocally ruled out Robert the Fleming, the eponymous founder of the parish of Roberton in the mid-twelfth century, as its builder, and instead pointed to Mary of Stirling as the person responsible. Mary's allegiance had been with the Balliols throughout the troubles but in 1346 she felt it necessary to resign her Roberton lands in the hope of securing a pardon from David II. The little motte overlooking a winding in the River Clyde seems to have been her way of defending herself and those in her service at such a critical time.

We saw earlier (page 17) that many of the 300-odd mottes recorded in Scotland are to be found in Galloway and Moray, and that hitherto this concentration has been put down to the fact that both regions were hostile to the crown in the twelfth and early thirteenth centuries. But both areas were also very turbulent during the early fourteenth century when the conflict was as much a civil war as a war of independence, with Bruce and his supporters set against Balliol's henchmen. With Roberton now dated to the early fourteenth century, it begs the question just how many other mottes in these regions might conceivably be of the same vintage. The oft-used distribution map of Scottish mottes may be more misleading than revealing.

After the wars were over

The return to Scotland in 1357 of King David II, Robert Bruce's son, from his lengthy captivity in England brought to an end the bloody wars with England. A greater part of the country had effectively been free of the English aggressor for some time, particularly the north and west, although a large swathe of southern Scotland still remained under their control, ruled from the castles situated at Roxburgh and Lochmaben. The return of a sort of peace was the time for all to rebuild their lives, and their homes.

In all wars there are winners and losers. In the wars with England the losers were the Balliols and their supporters, particularly the Comyns. The winners were those who had sided with Bruce, such as the Stewarts, Campbells and Douglases. The Douglases had been modest Lanarkshire landowners in the thirteenth century, but the close friendship between 'the Good' Sir James Douglas and King Robert Bruce secured their rise to the top. Through him they acquired substantial estates across the land, among them the barony of North Berwick, on the East Lothian coast. Sir James' beneficiary at his death in 1330 was his nephew, William. It was he who built mighty Tantallon Castle.

Tantallon – last of the great curtain-wall castles

The motive for William embarking on such a mammoth undertaking may have been prompted by his elevation to the peerage as the first earl of Douglas in 1358; certainly the castle has the hallmark of being a declaration of his new-found status. It was as if William Douglas consciously chose to look back to the golden age of castle building in the preceding century, and Tantallon can claim to be the last of the great curtain-walled castles built from new in Scotland.

The most important and conspicuous element in Tantallon's design was the awesome curtain of red sandstone drawn across the neck of the grassy headland (**36**). Impressively solid behind its yawning rock-cut ditch, it now has a somewhat careworn appearance, having been battered not only by cannon but also by the winds and storms that are as much a part of this exposed spot as the rugged cliffs themselves. The brute frontal mass of the curtain has just a few narrow slits lighting the wall chambers and access stairs behind. Three towers projecting from the great curtain provided the main residential accommodation. The central tower housed the gateway at ground level and four upper floors, part of which would almost certainly have been occupied by the constable. The north tower, known as the Douglas Tower, is of such a size (it had seven floors) that it must have been the earl's residence, his donjon. This is confirmed by the presence immediately behind it of a two-storey hall block, originally provided with halls on both floors, a great hall on the upper floor reserved for the lord's use, and a laigh (lower) hall for less-exalted gatherings. In essence, Tantallon was a Bothwell or a Kildrummy adapted to a promontory site, nothing more nothing less.

Tantallon was quite exceptional, and we shall never really know what motivated the earl of Douglas to build in the manner, and on the scale, that he did. In so doing, he was out of step with his peers, who were demonstrating a preference for a less ambitious and less costly residence, centred on the tower house. Even William himself at another of his seats, Hermitage, close by the Border with England, opted for the latest fashion, albeit in a rather unusual way.

36 The awesome curtain wall at Tantallon Castle, built about 1360 by William, first earl of Douglas, rears up behind the gun tower built by Archibald Douglas, sixth earl of Angus, prior to King James V's great siege in 1528.

Tall storeys – the re-emergence of the tower house

There was nothing new about the tower house. The stone towers that had sprung up in Orkney and Caithness in the twelfth century, and the timber towers that had been erected in ringworks and on top of mottes across the rest of the country, had led the way. The squat stone tower built in the early fourteenth century on the summit of the motte at Duffus may simply have been a re-creation in masonry of its timber predecessor. Perhaps our perception of the tower house as essentially a product of the fourteenth century is coloured by the surviving upstanding stone masonry. If all those timber towers built in the twelfth and thirteenth centuries had survived, would we now be talking of a new direction in castle-building, or simply of a new material for constructing them?

It may be that the free-standing tower as a lordly residence never actually declined during the thirteenth century, as has been claimed, but simply that certain magnates were persuaded to build anew in the grand manner. Perhaps we should not be asking why the tower house re-emerged in the fourteenth century but why the curtain-walled castle went out of favour so soon? Various theories have been advanced for the resurgence of the tower house, including financial impoverishment following years of war, the 'down-sizing' of baronial households, and the failure of the mighty castles to withstand siege. Perhaps the answer is a combination of all three, and others besides.

The prevailing view of the tower-house castle is of a lofty, isolated dwelling housing all its lord's residential needs. If the tower was accompanied by other buildings, these were in the nature of 'farmyard attachments' and not buildings that any self-respecting lord would deign to enter. Such a picture might be a more accurate reflection of the tower houses of the sixteenth and seventeenth centuries, when the social order was very different, but it cannot be sustained for those erected in the fourteenth and fifteenth centuries. Once again, the misconception is brought about by our obsession with the upstanding masonry, and our failure to take into account what has vanished from our sight and is now only recoverable through excavation of the site. To quote an old adage: absence of evidence is not necessarily evidence of absence.

Excavations at Threave

The tall, forbidding tower that dominates the little island of Threave in the Kirkcudbrightshire Dee is the most impressive of all these early towers (**40**). It was built for Archibald Douglas 'the Grim' (so-called by the English, it was said, 'becaus of his terrible countenance in weirfair') following his elevation to the lordship of Galloway in 1369.

Before the excavations in the 1970s, the prevailing view of Threave was of a mighty tower house standing in splendid isolation on its island – 'a tower and nothing but a tower'. But was this sufficient for someone of Archibald Douglas's standing, who at his death was the most powerful nobleman in southern Scotland? How, for example, did it compare with the amount of accommodation available to his cousin, William Douglas, at Tantallon?

37 The gaunt, forbidding ruin of Threave Castle from across the River Dee. Within a century of Archibald 'the Grim', third earl of Douglas, building the castle, around 1370, all the buildings surrounding the tower house were demolished and replaced by the existing artillery fortification, in preparation for the 'showdown' between the Black Douglases and the royal house of Stewart.

The answer is: very badly. A conservative estimate of the floor space at Tantallon, counting only those buildings currently standing, comes to about 1,100sq m (12,000sq ft), over double that at Threave. Not only that, but the amount available in the Douglas Tower at Tantallon, identified as the earl's private lodging within the castle, adds up to 450sq m (5,000sq ft), the same as Threave. Were we then missing something at the latter?

38 Threave Castle, near Castle Douglas, Kirkcudbrightshire, from the north in 1976. The two buildings found close beside Archibald the Grim's tower house were built contemporaneously with the tower in the later fourteenth century but were demolished about 1450 to make room for the new artillery fortification that was wrapped around the tower house.

The excavations clearly showed that we were. Under the grass to the east of the tower house, within metres of Archibald's front door, were found the masonry foundations of two substantial structures of fourteenth-century date (**38**). Both were interpreted as being of two storeys, in which case taken together they add a further 600sq m (6,500sq ft) of living space, thereby matching almost exactly the provision at Tantallon. The excavations by no means exhausted all the extra accommodation around the tower house, just as at Tantallon there must be more to be found.

The excavations did not enable the functions of the two buildings to be identified, but by analogy with other sites, such as Archibald's other chief seat at rebuilt Bothwell, we might postulate a great hall for the one and extra lodging space, including possibly a chapel, for the other. Black Archibald's residence now takes on a very different appearance to the lonely tower house there today. Thanks to the excavations we can picture most of the habitable part of the island crammed with buildings, two of which at least were of high status (**39**). In this regard the castle complex begins to take on an appearance similar to that at Finlaggan, the principal residence on Islay of the MacDonald Lords of the Isles, who rose to prominence about the same time as the Douglases (**40**). There, two islands linked by a causeway were crowded with an assortment of buildings, including over twenty on the larger Eilean Mor. The only significant difference between the two complexes is the nature of the lord's private residence, for that at Finlaggan seems not to have been a tower house.

Threave and the other fourteenth-century towers might now be seen in a different light from hitherto – not so much castles in their own right but private lodgings reserved for the lord's own use, and the last resort in times of trouble, set within a much larger complex which more sensibly matches our understanding of the nature of baronial obligations and the size and scale of their households. We might reasonably christen them tower-house castles, to distinguish them from the curtain-walled castles of the preceding century. In the latter, the dominating feature had been the mighty enclosing wall, and the accommodation, with the exception of the great hall, had been firmly embedded within it. In the tower-house castle, the curtain was reduced to a perimeter wall of middling strength, playing second fiddle to the lordly accommodation. The perfect illustration of this is Doune Castle.

Doune – the perfect tower-house castle

Doune, beside the River Teith 12km (7½ miles) north-west of Stirling, was built towards the end of the century by Robert Stewart, first duke of Albany, earl of Menteith and Fife, and the younger brother of Robert III. From 1388 until his death in 1420 he was the effective ruler of the kingdom, Scotland's 'uncrowned king', and his seat at Doune virtually a royal castle. What we see there today was planned and executed in a single building programme, though the original scheme was never fully completed (see **41**).

Albany's vision was of four ranges of buildings set around a central court. The

39 *How Threave Island might have looked at the time of Archibald the Grim's death there in 1400, based on the excavated evidence and illustrated by David Simon. This image of a bustling island community contrasts dramatically with the present perception of an isolated tower house.*

40 *Plan of Finlaggan, the island residence of the MacDonald Lords of the Isles on Islay, Argyllshire.*

principal range along the north and north-west sides was to dominate all else. To achieve this it took the place of the perimeter wall, while the other ranges were to be built against the inside face of that defensive wall in the more traditional manner. This main range is as perfect a piece of medieval castle planning as one will find anywhere.

A lofty tower, the gate tower, at the east end provided the duke and duchess with a spacious four-storey apartment, similar in size to Threave. It had its own defended courtyard entrance, and independent access from its first-floor hall into the dais end of the great hall to its west. The voluminous great hall itself, set upon cavernous storage vaults, had a separate entrance at its lower 'screens' end. Adjacent to the great hall, and linked to it by a servery, was the kitchen tower, more modest in size than the gate tower but housing an impressive kitchen on the first floor and two floors of respectable lodging space above. Interestingly, the amount of floor space in the range totals some 1,100sq m (12,000sq ft), identical to that at Tantallon and Threave.

It is Doune's cathedral-like great hall that impresses most today (**42**). It measures 170sq m (1,830sq ft) and rises 11m (36ft) to the apex of the roof. There are no fireplaces, so iron braziers must have heated the assembled throng summoned to sup with Albany, a man noted for his 'large tabling and belly cheer'. Its existence is a reminder of the continuing, pivotal importance of the great hall in castle planning.

42 *The cathedral-like great hall in Doune Castle. The room was restored, and the present roof put on, by the fourteenth earl of Moray in 1883, but evidence existed for the central brazier stance and the round-headed doorway at the far end that led to Albany's private apartment in the tower beyond.*

The great hall at Darnaway

The number of more-or-less complete great halls surviving in Scotland can be counted on the fingers of one hand, and even that at Doune owes its present appearance to the intervention of the fourteenth earl of Moray in the 1880s, who restored it. By happy coincidence there exists at the earl of Moray's main seat, Darnaway (Morayshire), one of only two medieval great halls in the country still with its original roof (the other is in Edinburgh Castle).

The roof over 'Randolph's Hall' at Darnaway used to be ascribed on art-historical grounds to the 1450s, but recent dendrochronology has unequivocally placed its construction in the year 1387, making it earlier than the great hammer-beam roof over Westminster Hall, London, by several years (**43**). Darnaway's owner at the time was John Dunbar, earl of Moray and a brother-in-law of the king. The roof is a marvellous example of medieval craftsmanship. Its unusual hammer-beam form is enlivened with

carved decoration. Two of the seven principal trusses are elaborately ornamented, possibly indicating the positions of partitions or screens in the open hall, demarcating the dais and service areas. In addition, there is a wealth of carving – human figures, birds and beasts – inhabiting the structure. Of particular interest are the human figures on the ends of some of the hammer beams. These include two crowned male heads facing each other on the principal truss, a pair of cloaked and hooded clerics part way down (**44**), and, 'below the salt', a lustful male, with a twinkle in his eye and an erect penis, gazing across the hall into the doleful eyes of the welcoming sow opposite!

All in all, the roof is a remarkable legacy, giving us a fascinating glimpse into the Scotland of Archibald 'the Grim' and his contemporaries. It is a comfort to know that, after almost a century of war with England, the Scots had lost neither their sense of humour, nor their love of nature.

43 *Part of the hammer-beam roof over 'Randolph's Hall' at Darnaway Castle, whose great oak trusses have been dated to the year 1387, making it earlier than the great roof over Westminster Hall, London, by several years.*

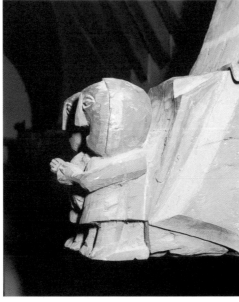

44 *The pair of clerics carved on one of the hammer-beam ends in 'Randolph's Hall', Darnaway Castle.*

Artefacts and aspects of castle life

The carved heads high up in 'Randolph's Hall' represent one insight into castle life; artefacts recovered from below the ground during excavation shed light on others.

The importance of the horse is evident through the abundance of horse trappings, such as spurs, harness pendants, bits and shoes. Horses were used for work and leisure more than they were for war, and many of the arrowheads found would have been for use in the hunt rather than in fighting. Dice, chess-pieces and counters illustrate other leisure pursuits. Other items of personal equipment frequently found include knives and daggers, spoons, personal seal matrices and assorted items of jewellery. Household artefacts commonly found include barrel padlocks, keys of various kinds, candle holders and oil-lamp bowls, iron and bronze cauldrons, pottery and other vessels of glass and, very occasionally, of wood. Undoubtedly the finest collection of wooden bowls and platters came from the little harbour at Threave (**45**).

Thanks to its waterlogged conditions, which ensured the survival of organic as well as inorganic material, Threave harbour produced a far more representative sample of castle artefacts than any other Scottish castle. The picture that emerged from the harbour mud was of a community largely self-sufficient in the production of wooden objects, leather goods, iron, lead and even glass. Interestingly, given the predominance of the material at other excavations, the islanders seemed to have little need of pottery.

From the harbour mud at Threave emerged another type of artefact, and in quantity, thirty-four stone cannonballs. They serve to illustrate that life on the island, indeed throughout the whole of Scotland, was to be vulnerable to a new threat as the new century dawned.

45 A wooden platter and bowl found in the harbour mud at Threave Castle in 1976. Most of the platters and bowls had the Douglas 'heart' branded into the undersides of their bases – an armorial device adopted by the family in recognition of 'the Good' Sir James's exploits with the heart of King Robert the Bruce following his death in 1329.

4

The coming of the gun: the fifteenth century

In that year [1436], King James raised a very strong army and besieged Roxburgh Castle about the beginning of the month of August. There were in number more than two hundred thousand men-at-arms. But they waited there a fortnight doing nothing worth recording because of a detestable split and most unworthy difference arising from jealousy; so, after losing all their fine large guns, both cannon and mortars, and gunpowder and carriages and wagons and many other things utterly indispensable for a siege, they returned home most ingloriously without effecting their object.

A new menace

The account of James I's abortive attempt to wrest Roxburgh Castle back from the English, described in the near-contemporary *Book of Pluscarden*, is clearly greatly exaggerated; we cannot imagine for one moment that a fifth of the entire population of the country was at the siege! Also, the impression given of a mighty artillery train seems to be hyperbole for the sake of effect. But that the Scots had guns at their disposal on that occasion is not in dispute.

Gunpowder artillery had appeared in Western Europe by the early fourteenth century, and the Scots were not slow in realizing its potential. Primitive pieces might have been among the armament deployed against Dundarg Castle (Aberdeenshire) in 1334 and Stirling Castle in 1337. Before the end of the century Edinburgh Castle, by then already the location of a small armaments industry making bows, crossbows and siege engines, seems also to be emerging as an arsenal for the new-fangled weapon; in 1384 'an instrument called a gun' was purchased for the fortress, together with quantities of sulphur and saltpetre for making the gunpowder.

46 Mons Meg, on display in Edinburgh Castle. The mighty muzzle-loaded bombard, manufactured in 1449, weighed over 6040kg (6 tons) and fired gunstones weighing 150kg (350lbs) a distance of almost 3km (2 miles).

By now an 'arms race' was developing across the states and principalities of Western Europe in which the Scottish monarchs played their part. By the time of James II's death in 1460, at yet another siege of Roxburgh, this one ultimately successful, the royal artillery train was considerable, pride of place going to a giant siege gun, or bombard, called 'Mons' (or Mons Meg as she came to be known), gifted in 1457 by the king's uncle-by-marriage, Duke Phillip of Burgundy (**46**). But bombards proved to be inordinately cumbersome beasts, both to trundle about the country (Mons could cover only 5km [3 miles] a day) as well as to fire (Mons fired perhaps eight stones a day, such was the enormous heat generated in her breech after each firing). Their transportation was also a huge drain on resources. As a result, by the end of the fifteenth century the bombard had effectively been pensioned off (Mons became a ceremonial saluting gun) and replaced by smaller, more manageable pieces. Even then, the gun cannot be said to have achieved final supremacy over the more conventional armament until well into the sixteenth century. Nevertheless, as the fifteenth century wore on, builders of castles had no option but to take the new firearm into account.

Peace with security

This talk of guns might lead the reader into thinking that the Scots throughout the later Middle Ages were constantly at war, either with each other or with the English. This is after all the traditional, post-Jacobite view of late medieval Scotland, as a country of 'barbarous Scots' riven by 'the usual amount of feudal tyranny, violations of law and outrages on humanity'. However, this perception of a country torn apart by outbreaks of violence, wherein feeble kings failed to control their overbearing barons, is simply not borne out by the facts, as Grant has recently demonstrated: 'Between 1341 and 1469 no Scottish king was overthrown by political opponents, whereas two were in England; England experienced twice as many rebellions and three times as many civil war battles; and three times as many English magnates met politically-related deaths, although the Scottish and English magnate classes were much the same size.'

That the Scots continued to build castles long after most of their English counterparts had ceased to do so has been taken as confirmation that Scottish domestic politics was far more turbulent than that prevailing south of the Border. This corresponds neatly with the widely held belief that all castles were built in times of trouble, that they were primarily defensive. But can we really sustain the argument that life was so troubled in late-medieval Scotland that many landowners were forced to build costly fortified residences in stone solely in order to defend themselves and those in their charge?

Looking down the other end of the telescope it could as easily be argued that the castle-building boom of the fifteenth century was rather more a reflection of the country's political stability and of the growing confidence of the nobility in its future. Building in stone and lime was a specialized, and costly, operation, not something that could be undertaken in haste. It required a considerable investment of capital spread over a number of years. No self-respecting nobleman was going to rush into such a venture unless he had a reasonable prospect of seeing it completed, and thereafter enjoying the fruits of his endeavours. For that he needed settled political conditions, and confidence that he had secure title to the land. The late-medieval castle, far from being regarded as an indicator of a disordered society, should more realistically be seen as a sign of peace and prosperity, where a nobleman's concern was as much for prestige and comfort as it was for security.

The rise of the middling sort

47 An impression of how the tower house in Cardoness Castle, Kirkcudbrightshire, might have been used by the McCullochs in the later fifteenth century (David Simon).

The building of costly stone residences had up till then largely been the preserve of the monarchy and the senior nobility. It has been estimated that of the 2,000 heads of noble families in Scotland in about 1300, no more than fifty could be regarded as magnates. The remainder, while still classed as nobility, would be more accurately termed 'landed gentry'. But by 1400 the picture was changing. The crown, for example, was already eroding the power of the provincial earldoms and important lordships that had dominated society up till then, and an act of 1401 ensured that when these came into the crown's possession, any baronies within them would henceforth be held directly of the crown. The number of 'tenants-in-chief' increased as a result.

This rise of the middling sort throughout the fifteenth century is reflected in the castle boom. More and more landowners, emboldened through their elevated status as tenants of the crown, and encouraged by the knowledge that they held their land 'in feu and heredity and in perpetuity', now chose to 'move up-market' and invest their capital in new buildings. There was no legal impediment preventing them from doing so; in Scotland all freeholders were equal under the law. The only social barrier to their building a stone castle seems to have been a financial one.

Cardoness – a typical tower house

The majority of these new castles took the lofty tower-house form rather than that of the more modest hall-house variety. Cardoness Castle (Kirkcudbrightshire), built about 1475 by the McCullochs, a powerful Galloway family, was typical (**47**). The rectangular building rose 17m (56ft) to the battlements. Once through the ground-level front door, one was confronted with six floors of accommodation arranged in a similar fashion to that at Threave – that is, service rooms at the bottom, a fine lord's hall in the middle, and private chambers at the top. These were reached by a spiral stair placed beside the entrance at one corner of the rectangle. Clever use was made of the 3m (10ft) thick walls to carve out small side chambers at every level. These served a variety of uses, including a guardroom, a prison and pit, and several closets for use either as bedchambers, wardrobes or latrines. The hall was particularly finely detailed, with an attractive fireplace, an exquisite aumbry (cupboard) where the laird's finest plate would be displayed, and pretty stone window-seats. The available floor space amounted to about 320sq m (3,444sq ft), two-thirds that of Threave, reflecting the more lowly status of its owner.

Cardoness does not stand alone, but has the remains of buildings surviving in its shadow. It is impossible to determine what function they served but my guess is that one would have been a great hall, to complement the provision within the tower house. The lordly obligations of the McCullochs would not have been as onerous or as elaborate as those of someone like Archibald 'the Grim', but that would not have removed the necessity for such a public reception space. Evidence from other tower-house castles in Scotland confirms that these later tower houses, even those belonging to quite modest lairds, were not intended to house all the noble functions.

Towers and halls

The hall (*aula*), the principal reception room in a nobleman's house, had been at the heart of castle planning from the very outset. That it continued to play an important part in late-medieval castle planning in Scotland is attested in both the surviving documentation – the phrase 'to build a house with a hall' occurs in about fifty feu charters during James IV's reign (1488–1513) – and the standing buildings themselves. The hall provided a suitably impressive space in which its lord could carry out his courtly and social obligations; more than any other room in the castle complex, it reflected in its sheer size and elaborate ornamentation its owner's social standing and aspirations.

Castle Campbell (Clackmannanshire) was begun by Colin Campbell, first earl of Argyll, in the 1460s to serve as his chief Lowland seat (**48**). His principal residence (which no longer exists) was at Inveraray, in Argyllshire. By the time of his death in 1493, he had created the perfect tower-house castle, which still stands remarkably intact. The tower house, standing over 20m (66ft) high, still dominates the site, as it was always intended to. Its four floors and garret served as the earl's private apartment – over 200sq m (2150sq ft) of floor space, arranged just as at Cardoness.

Across the courtyard from the tower house was Earl Colin's great hall, on the first floor above a range of storage cellars. It was in this spacious great hall, rather than in the cramped surroundings of his own hall in the tower house, where the earl could entertain in fine style and impress his noble guests. It measured 15m by 9m, had a generous fireplace, and a row of good-sized windows facing south and giving majestic views over the castle's formal gardens and across the Forth valley to the Pentland Hills. It was flanked on one side by the kitchen, and on the other by a withdrawing room, to which the earl and his most favoured guests could retire when they so desired. Overlooking the courtyard to the north was a fine timber gallery (now gone).

The Pringles of Smailholm Tower (Roxburghshire) weren't quite in the same class as the Campbells. The head of the family was a squire of the earl of Douglas, who managed a part of the Ettrick Forest on his lordship's behalf. The position, however, brought with it both status and wealth, which perhaps explains why the family chose to build in costly stone and lime. Their modest, five-storey rectangular tower, providing 200sq m (2,150sq ft) of floor space, testifies to their more lowly lairdly status. However, recent excavations in the barmkin surrounding the tower house uncovered evidence for a hall block, in this case of single storey height, to complement the cramped accommodation in the tower (**49**). The block consisted of a hall measuring 50sq m (538sq ft) nearer to the outer gateway, and a chamber half that size at the end closer to the tower house. The hall was heated by a brazier placed in the centre of the room, in a manner identical to the much grander great hall at Doune. Across the courtyard from the hall was the two-roomed kitchen block.

Until these excavations, the absence of kitchens within the tower houses themselves had been put down to several factors, most popular being the fire risk and the undesirable smells. Yet the tower houses of the senior nobility generally had kitchens; Archibald 'the Grim' evidently wasn't overly bothered about either going up in flames or being overwhelmed by the stink of cabbage water wafting up the stairs! The more likely explanation for the lack of kitchens in the lesser tower houses, such as Cardoness and Smailholm, is that, with space at a premium, the cooking of private family meals was done over the hall fire, as numerous contemporary woodcuts suggest; more public feasts were catered for in the kitchen beside the outer hall.

The excavations at Threave demonstrated that the mighty tower house of a great late fourteenth-century magnate was but the central element in a much more elaborate complex of buildings, the lord's private residence and place of last resort. The excavations at Smailholm show how that same picture can be carried forward into the fifteenth century, and down the social ladder.

Variations on a theme

The single most appealing feature of the Scottish tower house as a building type is its considerable variety. Builders took the original simple rectangular form and stretched it, added to it and contorted it into all shapes and sizes. No two towers were identical, though they all had features in common. The castle 'boom' of the fifteenth century began this process of mutation in earnest, a development that lasted until well into the seventeenth century.

The tower houses that we have encountered up to now have all been of the rectangular form, and most tower houses built during the century were similarly contrived. The most common variation on this theme was the L-plan where a smaller jamb (or wing) was attached to one side of the main block. Depending on its size, the jamb could be used for a number of purposes.

At Affleck Castle (Angus), built towards the end of the century by one of the Auchinleck family, the jamb was just a sixteenth the size of the main block and was utilized in its lower storeys for the main spiral stair giving access to the hall on the third floor. Thereafter, the stair to the upper levels and the battlements was carried up in a spiral contained in the thickness of one of the other corners, freeing up the remaining two floors of the jamb as living space. The lower one, entered by steps off the hall, may have served as a bedchamber for the steward; the upper level, entered off the laird's private chamber, housed a lovely little chapel (**50**).

50 The charming little chapel in the tower house at Affleck, north of Dundee, Angus. It was entered off the laird's private chamber.

Affleck's plan is unusual for this period. The more normal arrangement was to apply a much bigger jamb to the main block and use the greater floor space to provide a more flexible arrangement of the accommodation. The tower house at Neidpath Castle (Peeblesshire), built at the beginning of the century by the Hays of Locherworth, ancestors of the earls of Tweeddale, had a jamb just one quarter the size of the main block. It was entirely devoted to living space, including a pit-prison at ground level, a storeroom on the first floor, a kitchen off the hall and private chambers on the top two levels.

One tower house, Orchardton Tower (Kirkcudbrightshire), was unique in Scotland in being circular in form, although the rooms inside were square on plan (**51**). The Cairns family, who built it about the middle of the century, must have had

an Irish connection for the form is more common on the other side of the North Channel, for example Synone (County Tipperary). In all other respects, Orchardton follows the standard layout of accommodation, with a cellar at ground level (independently accessed), a hall on the first floor and private chambers above. Orchardton also provides a good example of the relationship between the private tower house and the more public hall block, which lies adjacent.

Borthwick – a most unusual tower house

Of all the tower houses built during the century, one in particular, Borthwick Castle (Midlothian), stands out from the rest for a whole variety of reasons: for its monumental size – at a height of 36m (118ft) it was the loftiest; for its massive scale – with a total floor space in excess of 1,100sq m (12,000sq ft) it was the largest; for the supreme quality of its ashlar construction; and for the very clever arrangement of the accommodation. Sir William Borthwick, who in 1430 received a licence from James I 'to construct a castle . . . and to erect and fortify the same', must have been pleased with what he built, and greatly admired (and envied) by his peers. Yet Sir William was only in the second rank of the nobility at the time he created it; it would be twenty years before he was elevated to the new peerage established by James II and given the title of Lord Borthwick, thereby raising him to the top rank. Evidently, Sir William was a man determined to better himself.

The sheer volume of Borthwick strongly suggests that Sir William was contriving to bring all his lordly accommodation under one roof, rather than have two or perhaps three high-status buildings in close proximity to each other, as Archibald 'the Grim' had produced at Threave. In this, Sir William was not being entirely innovative. Hermitage Castle, begun by Archibald's cousin, William, first earl of Douglas, and completed by his successors before 1400, achieved a similar result, albeit by stages and not at one fell swoop. So too did the tower house built inside the twelfth-century ringwork at Crookston by Sir John Stewart of Darnley about 1400 (see **4**). Unfortunately, both castles defy proper analysis.

At Hermitage, the 'restoration work' of the early nineteenth century removed much of the evidence, while at Crookston most of the main block and western towers have long since disappeared, possibly as a result of the punishment meted out by Mons Meg during the 1489 siege. Nevertheless, enough remains at both sites to hint that their central blocks housed the public rooms, including the great hall and withdrawing chamber, while the four projecting jambs, one at each corner, contained all the other accommodation one would expect to find in a conventional tower house.

The arrangement at Borthwick is not so convoluted (**52**). The main block had just two jambs projecting from it, both from the same side and flush with the gable walls to create a kind of E-plan without the central stem. Storerooms took up the ground and first floors. On the second floor was the splendid great hall (**53**), measuring 112sq m (1,200sq ft) and rising 10m (33ft) to the apex of its great stone vault, with the withdrawing chamber and kitchen in the two adjacent jambs. The upper floors comprised the lordly apartments, including a good-sized hall (as big and as impressive as one would find anywhere else in the country at the time) and a chapel.

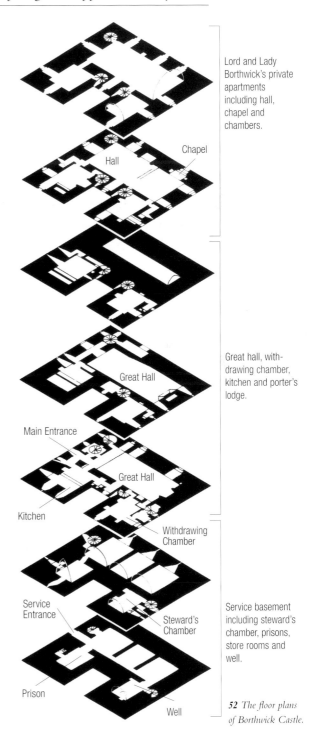

Lord and Lady Borthwick's private apartments including hall, chapel and chambers.

Hall   Chapel

Great hall, withdrawing chamber, kitchen and porter's lodge.

Great Hall

Main Entrance

Great Hall

Kitchen

Withdrawing Chamber

Service Entrance

Steward's Chamber

Service basement including steward's chamber, prisons, store rooms and well.

Prison

Well

52 The floor plans of Borthwick Castle.

Masons and their marks

Borthwick holds another potential treasure, for cut into its ashlar-block walls is a liberal sprinkling of masons' marks, over sixty different marks in total. I use the word 'potential' because to date there has been little research done on Scottish masons' marks. This is to be regretted for a more thorough analysis could achieve several ends. It could lead to a better building chronology within a specific castle, and it could link the construction of different buildings, not just castles, with the same group of masons. Zeune has recently ably demonstrated this rich potential, and what follows is the fruit of his research.

The masons' marks in Borthwick enabled the tower house to be analysed from bottom to top. Several facts emerged. Most significant was confirmation that the structure was of homogenous build. The spiral stairs, doors, windows, fireplaces, closets, vaults, the kitchen arch, the fireplace, basin and buffet in the great hall, the chapel, even the curb on the basement well, were all original.

Only the odd window enlargement, door insertion, fireplace restoration, stair repair and garret rebuilding were shown to be of later date. Secondly, the individual mason was versatile, at one time producing a newel-tread for one of the spiral stairs, at another hewing an elaborately carved piece for the great hall buffet. The study also demonstrated that there was a fair amount of coming and going by the masons, including the interesting observation that for the construction of the impressive stone vault over the great hall, several new masons were brought on site who worked on that one feature alone.

What then of the possibility of linking the masons who contributed to the building of Borthwick with other building projects? Zeune once again suggests some intriguing possibilities. Some twenty of the masons who worked on Borthwick also created Roslin Chapel, perfectly understandable given the close proximity of the two sites and the fact that the building of the chapel followed neatly the completion of the castle. But other masons working on Roslin had travelled from much further afield, including several from Angus, where they had been engaged in building work at two castles, Airlie and Inverquharity, as well as Arbroath Abbey. From Roslin, masons travelled to a variety of building sites, including Melrose Abbey (Roxburghshire), Linlithgow Palace, Ravenscraig Castle and Rosyth Castle (both Fife), Dean Castle (Ayrshire) and the Campbell stronghold at Kilchurn on Loch Awe (Argyllshire).

Scarcely anything is known about the master-masons and masons themselves, or for that matter the army of joiners, slaters, glaziers, smiths and labourers who contributed so much to the castle boom of the fifteenth century. Even their names are a mystery. The only master-masons of this century known to us by name are Henry Merlion, who was engaged by the crown at Ravenscraig in the early 1460s, Walter Merlion, his son, who worked on Stirling Castle and the Palace of Holyroodhouse, Andrew Aytoun, who was also employed at Stirling Castle, John French, who worked on Linlithgow Palace, and the Frenchman, John Morow, who thoughtfully placed an account of his works, none of them castles apparently, on a wall in Melrose Abbey. The quality of their creations is testimony to their craftsmanship, the quantity to their hard work. The end of a finger discovered in 1974 between two stones forming the arched entranceway into the Hepburns' castle of Hailes, beside the East Lothian Tyne, is silent testimony to the fact that their working conditions were not without hazard.

Home improvements

The masons and other craftsmen were engaged not only on building new stone castles but also on upgrading existing residences.

The most obvious candidates in urgent need of improvement were those mighty curtain-walled castles erected in the 'golden age' of the thirteenth century when great magnates had grand ideas — and required just as grand households to sustain them. By the fifteenth century, such residences were obsolete, the product of a bygone age, and more compact and comfortable lordly seats were increasingly the order of the day. They were also probably in need of urgent repair and attention, particularly given the punishment meted out to them during the bloody wars with England.

Take the Black Douglases, for example. Faced with the daunting prospect of rebuilding the shattered castle of Bothwell, acquired through marriage in the mid-fourteenth century, they ended up with a walled enclosure half the size of that

53 A nineteenth-century engraving of the great hall in Borthwick Castle, looking towards the dais end, with its grand fireplace and elaborate buffet recess (right). The artist, Robert Billings, has used the fireplace hood to highlight the many masons' marks.

originally contemplated by Walter of Moray. This was centred on a lofty tower house (now largely gone) and a great hall (largely complete to its wall-head), built during the time of Archibald, the fourth earl, in the early fifteenth century (**54**). Archibald's brother-in-law, Walter Halyburton, was similarly engaged in rebuilding an old fortress, Dirleton (see **20**), and he too chose to build an imposing tower-house residence in preference to the multi-towered complex of his illustrious de Vaux ancestor (**55**). It remains one of the great tragedies in Scottish architectural history that so little survives of his creation. We are left only with the basement of his tower house, with its pretty chapel above a particularly grim prison and pit, the cavernous storage vaults (**56**) beneath his great hall, and the cathedral-like kitchens. The great hall itself must have been a magnificent space if the stone buffet in the screens passage is anything to judge by.

Major rebuilding at the more venerable residences was motivated by necessity. A different motive lay behind home improvements to relatively new residences. No sooner had William Crichton come into possession of the tower-house castle built by his father than he embarked on a scheme to improve it. The most important element in his new castle was a splendid great hall along the south side of the courtyard, with the main entrance and cellars at ground level and the hall itself on the upper floor (**57**).

Crichton's motive can only have been a desire to display his own wealth and status, and he was very much a man on his way up in the world. A trusted servant of James I, by the time of the king's death in 1437 he had become sheriff of Edinburgh and keeper of the castle there. Two years later, he was elevated to the prestigious position of chancellor. A fine new banqueting hall in his castle was surely his way of

54 *Bothwell Castle from the air, showing the extent of the late fourteenth-century Douglas castle in relation to that originally envisaged by Walter of Moray in the middle of the preceding century. The Douglases' residence was centred on a lofty rectangular tower house and great hall (centre left). The mighty donjon of the Morays (bottom right), badly damaged during the wars with England, was patched up and probably used for ancillary accommodation.*

55 *How the Halyburtons' residence in Dirleton Castle, East Lothian, might have looked in 1450 (David Simon).*

56 *The cavernous storage vaults beneath the Halyburtons' residence in Dirleton Castle. Each storage bay was entered separately from the courtyard (left) through a securely barred doorway. The sheer size of these vaults hints at the lavish banquets that must have been held in the great hall above.*

57 The courtyard in Crichton Castle, viewed from inside the tower house. Chancellor Crichton's great hall is on the left, reached by a fine stone forestair. The kitchens were in the far range.

announcing to all and sundry that he had arrived at centre stage of Scottish political and social life. It has resonances with the new east range added to Linlithgow Palace by his king, James I, in the 1420s. The equally impressive collegiate church Crichton built nearby simply reinforced the message. This burning desire to flaunt new-found rank and status through new building was repeated by noblemen across the country. When, for example, Sir Andrew Lundy, lord of Balgonie Castle (Fife), was elevated to the post of lord high treasurer in 1496, he too marked the occasion by adding a new hall block to his family seat.

'All warlike apparatus for defence'

The impetus behind the castle boom might well have been the desire for prestige and comfort, but there was still the need for security. When William Keith, the marischal, embarked on his building of dramatic Dunnottar Castle (Kincardineshire) shortly before 1400, he wanted somewhere 'for the safe-keeping of his people and his goods'. A status symbol and somewhere warm were all well and good, but it wasn't all sweetness and light in late medieval Scotland, and in an age before banks were invented a nobleman's wealth had to be securely stored in his home.

The first licence to build a fortified residence was that granted by James I to James of Dundas of that Ilk and his heirs in 1424. Permission was given 'to build, construct, fortify and erect on high the tower or fortalice of Dundas in the manner of a castle with crenellations ('le kyrnelys') and other manifestations below and above, with walls and ditches appropriate to this sort of fortalice, according to the custom of the kingdom of Scotland'. The tower house at Dundas Castle (West Lothian) still stands almost in its entirety and is typical of the 'warlike apparatus' built into many of these fifteenth-century castles.

First, the tower house was built on the L-plan, with the entrance door positioned in the re-entrant angle of the main block where it could be 'covered', that is protected, from the jamb. This use of the re-entrant angle to provide flanking defence became standard practice in later tower houses but was not always employed at this date. At Preston Castle (East Lothian), built by the Hamiltons in about 1450, the two superimposed entrances, one leading into the basement and the other giving access into the hall, were positioned on the opposite side of the main block from the jamb. The two superimposed entrances at Borthwick also ignored the defensive potential of the flanking jambs. Dundas's dependence on a ground-floor entrance was also not uniform at this date, though it became the norm later. Presumably, the upper entrances at Borthwick and elsewhere were reached by timber forestairs, perhaps with a retractable element for better security.

Most doorways at this date, wherever they were positioned in a building, were provided with two barriers, a wooden door and an iron

yett (open cross-barred gate). In certain 'licences to fortify' of about this date, including one granted to Herbert Lord Maxwell for Mearns Castle (Renfrewshire) of 1449 and George, earl of Angus, for Broughty Castle (Angus) of 1454, special mention was made of these 'iron gates'. Usually, they were placed behind the wooden door to strengthen it; less frequently they were placed at the front. Dundas still retains its iron yett.

The licences to fortify almost invariably highlight the importance of the wall-head. At Mearns, for instance, the laird was authorized to erect on the top of it 'all warlike apparatus necessary for its defence', and the surviving triple row of projecting corbels that once supported the oversailing parapet, evenly spaced to allow the defenders to fire down through the gaps, are testimony that Lord Maxwell carried out this particular letter of the law. This form of wall-head defence, called a machicolation, only began to come into fashion in Scotland in the early fifteenth century, to replace the timber hoards of the previous century, evidence for which can be seen at Threave (see **37**) and Hermitage. Particularly fine machicolations may be seen on the top of the Douglas Tower in Bothwell Castle, built about 1420 by the fourth earl of Douglas, and on the inner curtain wall at Craigmillar Castle, the Prestons of Gorton's residence near Edinburgh (**58**). The dating of Craigmillar's machicolated wall remains a matter of debate (see pages 82–83), but somewhere around the middle of the fifteenth century seems the most likely.

Dundas also has a fine machicolation, but unlike the other examples quoted it also retains its crenellated, or indented, parapet, which was specifically mentioned in the licence. This was 'warlike apparatus' of long standing, of course. However, we might

58 The inner curtain wall at Craigmillar Castle, Edinburgh, with its attractive machicolated parapet and projecting round towers fitted with gunholes.

question how necessary such elaborate wall-head defences were to James of Dundas and his peers. Did they really need to go to such lengths merely to ward off intruders and troublesome neighbours? Would not a simple parapet with a wall-walk behind, as at Neidpath, perhaps complemented by a projecting stone box placed on the wall-head directly over the entrance, as at Lochranza, have sufficed (**59**)? Although such battlements were built ostensibly for defence – and the licences confirm by their language this 'defensive' message – they seem unwarranted for the circumstances of the time and it may be argued that they were provided more for show than for strength. There is no doubting their eye-catching quality.

Threave and the arrival of artillery defence

The provision of wall-head defences, iron yetts and the like were all designed to counter the threat posed by conventional weapons, chiefly crossbows and stone-hurling artillery. From the middle of the century that situation began to change as the new firearm, the gun, started to come into its own. Certainly the warlike James II, by the time of his tragic death at Roxburgh in 1460, had built up a considerable artillery train, and there is clear evidence that some of his mightier subjects were similarly amassing

59 The box-machicolation projecting from the front wall of Lochranza Castle, Arran. This simple device enabled the defenders to protect the entrance door below.

arsenals. Foremost among them were the Black Douglases.

One of the greatest upheavals in fifteenth-century Scotland was the fall of the house of Black Douglas. Both during the years leading up to the dénouement in 1455 and in its aftermath, this showdown between the monarchy and the realm's most powerful baronial family had major repercussions. One effect of the whole affair was that it provided the combatants with a theatre of war in which to experiment with the new-fangled weapon.

The final act in the drama unfolded at Threave Castle in the summer of 1455. By the time of James II's arrival at the siege in early July, all the other Douglas strongholds – from Lochindorb in the north to Douglas itself – had fallen, thanks largely to the king's artillery. These included 'the gret gun the quhilk a Frenchman schot richt wele' at the siege of Abercorn. This may have been the same 'great bombard' that was hauled in June, at great expense and no little inconvenience, from Linlithgow Palace to Threave; it was emphatically not Mons Meg for, contrary to local tradition, she did not arrive in the country until two years later. The siege dragged on for two months, during which time James, the ninth and last earl of Black Douglas, fled to England and entrusted his island fastness into the custody of the English king, Henry VI. King James, despairing of ever taking the castle by storm, was forced into bribing the garrison into surrendering.

The most likely explanation for the king's failure to wrest Threave Castle by force was the presence of the formidable artillery fortification that had been wrapped around the fourteenth-century tower house prior to the siege (see **37**). This structure, described as the 'artillery house' in 1458, was a most remarkable construction, without parallel anywhere else. It took the form of two stone walls, 5m (16ft) high, built at 90 degrees to each other. Three circular gun towers, one at the point where the two walls met and the others at either end, projected out into the surrounding water-filled ditch (**60**). A gateway protected by a drawbridge was built mid-way along one wall. The lengths of wall were battered, or sloped, externally in an attempt to reduce the impact of incoming gunstones, and were provided with vertical slits, for use presumably by archers armed with crossbows and longbows. There is evidence for a wall-walk accessed from timber staging. The gun towers were three-storeyed, the lower two storeys fitted with three gunholes each, some shaped like a dumb-bell and some like an inverted keyhole. The top level was open to the elements and had a more conventional crenellated parapet.

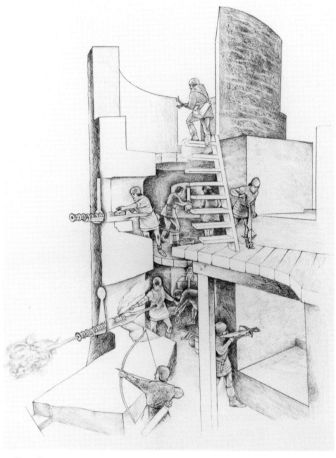

60 *How the central gun tower in Threave Castle's artillery wall might have been used during the 1455 siege (David Simon).*

In the early days of the siege, the earl of Douglas was accused of treason by king and parliament for fortifying and arming his castle of Threave. That they were compelled to act in this way because of the construction of this extraordinary artillery fortification received startling confirmation during excavations on the island in the 1970s. These showed that the two high-status buildings erected for Archibald 'the Grim' in front of his tower house had been demolished by the later fifteenth century, presumably to provide a clear field of fire for the gunners within the new fortification (see **38**). One of the gun towers also had an occupation level dated to the late fifteenth century. Moreover, a precise date of 1447 for the construction of the less substantial artillery wall along the riverside came from the tree-ring dating of the timber carrying the harbour gate. At this date William, the eighth earl, was still alive and the process of strengthening the island fastness against possible aggression seems to have been initiated by him. Following his murder at the king's own hand at Stirling Castle in 1452, the struggle was continued by his younger brother, James, the ninth earl. Clearly, the confrontation between Stewart and Douglas had been brewing for some considerable time.

Guns and gunholes

The precise nature of the guns the Douglases planned to poke through Threave's gunholes is not clear, though given the diameter of the apertures, 280mm (11in), they were clearly not bombards (Mons Meg had a muzzle 500mm [20in] across). A forged iron breech-loader, with a detachable chamber to hold the gunpowder charge, has been suggested. The barrel would have been bound to a wooden stock, which probably had a swivel-pin in its underside for fitting into a timber sill. Square holes in the sides of some of Threave's gunholes housed such sills. The numerous gunstones found in the harbour at Threave point to guns with calibres of 65 and 80mm (2½ and 3in), of a type known as 'serpentine'.

Threave's innovative freestanding artillery fortification, intended chiefly for use by guns against guns, was not followed in Scotland for another fifty years. The more usual approach was rather more conservative, simply providing castle walls with gunholes at strategic points. Even then, the number of castles so improved appears to have been quite small. The gunholes followed the two forms employed at Threave, with the 'inverted keyhole' type the more popular. Cardoness, not far from Threave Island, had four incorporated into its ground floor. The gatehouse into Newark Castle (Renfrewshire) had both types, although interestingly the tower house itself went without, the traditional simple slits deemed sufficient by the laird. By the end of the century, a third form of gunhole had joined them, the 'crosslet keyhole' type, though given its restricted distribution in the north east (at Ravenscraig in Aberdeenshire, and Arbuthnott and Glenbervie, both Kincardineshire) it was clearly just a regional variant.

There are two other castles, though, which appear to have had substantial artillery works carried out on them during the century, Craigmillar and Ravenscraig (Fife). The inner curtain wall with its four gun-looped projecting towers, wrapped around the early fifteenth-century L-plan tower house at Craigmillar, has already been mentioned on account of its splendid machicolated wall-head (see **58**). This feature, and an eighteenth-century reading of the date 1427 below the armorial over the entrance doorway, have previously led to the dating of the curtain wall to the first half of the century. Recently, that date has been called into question and a date in the early sixteenth century proposed, though the reasoning seems rather unconvincing. The towered curtain with its high, crenellated walls, however, has a very traditional 'medieval' feel about it, far more than Threave's innovative design, and it also served to provide extra castle accommodation. A date in the second quarter of the century seems perfectly acceptable. Given that gunholed structures were already well established elsewhere by 1400 (for example, in England at Bodiam Castle, Sussex, and in France at Blanquefort Castle), and given the date of Threave, there is no justification, on present evidence, for dating Craigmillar to a century later.

There is, though, more justification for calling into question the 1460–3 date for the works carried out at Ravenscraig but ordered by James II before his tragic death in 1460 (**61**). It used to be thought that, when that building programme was brought to a premature conclusion in 1463, the castle consisted of the two end towers but only the lower half of the central range. These parts incorporated keyhole gunholes. When the upper part of the central range was completed, to serve as a gun-platform rather than as a great hall as had originally been intended, wide-mouthed gunholes were introduced, indicating a date in the sixteenth century. A recent study of the masons' marks, however, strongly suggests that the only parts completed by 1463 were the east tower and the foundations of the central range, and the only keyhole gunhole there is clearly a later insertion. The rest of the ground floor of the central range and the whole of the west tower were built in a second phase, conceivably after the Sinclair earls of Orkney took possession of the castle after 1470. This might represent a mere decade of a difference, but it alters significantly our perception of Ravenscraig as a purpose-built artillery fortification.

61 Ravenscraig Castle, Kirkcaldy, Fife, from the north east, showing the various gunholes.

The loss of Berwick and the defence of the realm

It has been argued that the fortifications at Ravenscraig were part of a wider scheme designed to improve the coastal defences around the Firth of Forth. Certainly relations with England, never amicable even at the best of times, had begun to go awry again during James III's reign. The earl of Angus's raid into Northumberland in the summer of 1480 was the catalyst for renewed hostilities, and castles from St Andrews to Berwick-upon-Tweed were provisioned with men, victuals and artillery. In the late summer of 1482, the Scots' tenuous hold on Berwick-upon-Tweed finally came to an end, and the thriving settlement that had once been the country's chief town and port was ceded to the English. The brave defenders of the castle duly 'partit thairfra with bagg and baggages'.

One consequence of the fall of Berwick was the re-emergence of the royal castle at Dunbar, strategically positioned beside the natural invasion route into eastern Scotland. In 1496, James IV ordered a major reconstruction of the fortress, which included a new gatehouse and forework, part of which survives. The gunholes, of inverted keyhole type, confirm the documentary dating. But for some unexplained reason, the king's master mason chose to ignore the rocky promontory overlooking the forework and left it out of his scheme of defence. It was an oversight that was corrected only in the panic that followed King James' untimely death in 1513 on the bloody battlefield of Flodden in Northumberland. The new fortification heralded a new era for the castle in Scotland.

5

Garrisons and private homes: the sixteenth century

And finally touching the state and strenth of the castell of Dunbar whereof your grace is desirous to be advised, I assure your grace it is a thing in maner unprenable [unwinnable] for I have bene in it. It standith upon a crag and there is no waye to go to it but one which is strongly and substantially made with a new bulwerk and sett with ordinance as can be devised by the duke of Albany for in the said castell is all the duke's trust. And if the said bulwerk could be won I think there is no doubt but the castell might be won semblaby be reason that the said castell stands low upon a crag and the erth without it is hygh about it, and so there could nothing stint within it but the ordinance that were without the castell bete it.

Dunbar and the development of artillery defence

In November 1513, just twelve weeks after the disaster at Flodden, the Scots recognized John Stewart, duke of Albany, second in succession to the throne, as governor of the realm. Albany, then resident in France, arrived on Scottish soil in May 1515 and set up his headquarters at Dunbar. Lord Dacre's report to Cardinal Wolsey, despatched in June 1523, confirms the presence by that date of 'a new bulwerk' built in front of the royal fortress. That bulwark, or blockhouse, still exists, but only just, for

62 Dunbar Castle, East Lothian, from the west, with the town to the right. The blockhouse (centre left) was originally reached from the castle along a covered passage.

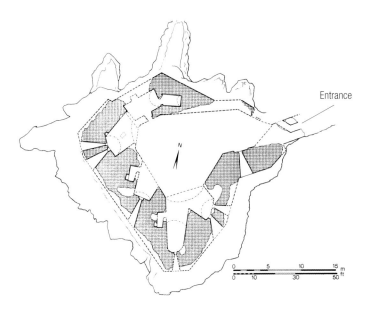

Entrance

*63 Plan of the Dunbar
blockhouse at
ground level.*

it clings like a limpet to the summit of an isolated rocky crag that is slowly crumbling into the sea. It was a fortification designed exclusively for gunpowder artillery, and can rightly claim to be the first of its type in Scotland, and among the first in the British Isles (**62**).

The blockhouse was positioned between the castle proper, on its seaward side, and the headland to the south. It was reached from the castle along a passage concealed within a traverse wall. The blockhouse itself was polygonal in plan, open to the rear and two storeys high (**63**). The massive walls at ground level, up to 6.5m (21ft) thick, were provided with four large, vaulted casemates serving six horizontal, wide-mouthed gunholes; a seventh gunhole was reached directly from the rear court. There was also some accommodation for the gunners. The upper level was open to the elements and fronted by a parapet wall 2m (6ft) thick. The ground-level gunholes, with circular throats up to 380mm (15in) across, point to their being used with sizeable pieces of artillery (a stocked breech-loader on a trestle mounting has been postulated). The upper tier of guns may have been longer-range muzzle-loaded pieces mounted on carriages; the emplacement was certainly wide enough for a heavy cannon to be run back.

The blockhouse was a remarkable structure for it broke new ground in artillery fortification, more so than Threave's artillery house had done fifty years earlier. The structure was clearly inspired from outside Scotland (the horizontal gunhole had appeared in France around 1460) and may well have been designed by Antoine d'Arces, Sieur de la Bastie, a French ambassador known to have been designing artillery works for Edinburgh Castle in 1514 and who was placed in charge of Dunbar in December of that year, to await Albany's coming. The horizontal, round-ended gunholes are the earliest datable examples in Scotland, and although the type did not entirely displace the more traditional, vertical, forms of gunhole, it very soon became the standard adopted throughout the country.

The blockhouse itself had a more restricted use. Archibald Douglas, sixth earl of Angus, couldn't quite see Dunbar from the safety of his ancestral seat at Tantallon, but he must surely have witnessed the building of its blockhouse for he attempted to imitate it shortly afterwards. The circular, two-storey gun tower and traverse wall beside the outer entrance into his castle is there yet (see **36**). The stub of another blockhouse, one of two grafted on to either end of the frontal curtain wall at St Andrews Castle in the 1520s, during James Beaton's episcopacy, hints at a structure of considerable strength and size. There is documentary evidence, though nothing surviving on the ground, for blockhouses further afield, including one built to guard the entrance to Aberdeen harbour.

In the basement gloom of the 'stern tower' in Blackness Castle, west of Edinburgh, are the remains of another awesome artillery fortification built at that royal castle in the late 1530s, a construction of such strength that even contemporaries were calling it 'formidable' and 'impregnable'. The 6m (20ft) thick wall at ground level was punctured by five great horizontal gunholes. The upper level was subsequently immured in a heightening of the wall but the remains can be seen of a crenellated parapet over which the heavier, carriage-mounted guns fired their murderous contents. The work was masterminded by Sir James Hamilton of Finnart, James V's master of works and one of the most remarkable men of his generation.

Hamilton's hideaway – Craignethan

Hamilton of Finnart had spent his early years abroad, learning about architecture and fortification, but had returned home to contribute to the bloody family feuds and to persecute those who would reform the Roman Church. He was a complicated soul; on the one hand a man of culture, a fine soldier and someone blessed with an outstanding grasp of architecture and military engineering, but on the other a bigot, a womanizer and one prone to great violence. His building legacy testifies to his complex personality. At Blackness, we see the dark side of his temperament, whereas at nearby Linlithgow Palace his majestic outer gate and pretty courtyard fountain proclaim his enlightened Renaissance credentials. Both sides are brought together to powerful and compelling effect at Craignethan Castle, the fortress-residence he built

64 How Sir James Hamilton of Finnart's masterpiece, Craignethan Castle, Lanarkshire, might have looked in 1550 (Tom Borthwick).

for himself in deepest Lanarkshire. Hamilton's hideaway was an articulate fusion of military and domestic architecture (**64**). It also proved to be the last great private fastness built from scratch in Scotland. The age of the Scottish castle can truly be said to have come to an end with Craignethan; henceforth there would be only fortified houses.

Craignethan was hidden away in a quiet, inaccessible position overlooking the Water of Nethan, a tributary of the Clyde. Around three sides of the spur on which it was built the ground fell steeply away. Clearly expecting little threat from these quarters, Finnart relied on a traditional medieval defence – rectangular towers projecting from the

angles and mid-points of the curtain wall. The only concessions to the new artillery were the horizontal gunholes for handguns and the 3m (10ft)-thick east rampart, facing onto the gorge, evidently designed to take heavier pieces in the manner of Dunbar and Blackness.

But it was the higher ground overlooking the spur from the west that presented the real defensive threat, and Finnart rose to the challenge. There he created a fortification of revolutionary form and incredible strength, consisting chiefly of a 5m (16ft)-thick stone rampart built across the spur. Sadly, the slighting of the castle in 1579 resulted in its demolition and we now have no way of determining either its full height or its detailed appearance. The reconstruction drawing attempts to convey an impression of its former grandeur; vaulted casemates for trestle-mounted guns at ground level, and a broad, crenellated parapet at the top for heavier, carriage-mounted cannon. The great, flat-bottomed ditch fronting the rampart does still exist, though it was only rediscovered 40 years ago, and in the bottom of that ditch was found Craignethan's most remarkable feature.

The caponier discovered in 1962 was a stone-vaulted, gunholed gallery from within which soldiers armed with handguns could rake the ditch (**65** and **66**). The name derived from the Italian *capannata*, meaning 'little hut', and the prototype was apparently invented in Italy, by Francesco di Giorgio Martini, about 1500. Caponiers had a very limited life at the time, and the only other sixteenth-century caponier surviving in Britain is, not surprisingly, at Blackness. The problem seems to have been the lack of ventilation in the cramped vault, for no sooner did the gunners fire off a volley than they were suffocated by gunpowder smoke.

Angle-bastioned fortifications

The Dunbar blockhouse and Craignethan's west rampart represented a new departure in artillery fortification for Scotland, and yet both were already outmoded when compared with military engineering on the continent. The Scottish works, like the Henrician fortresses built along the south coast of England about 1540, were really little more than an extension of the medieval tradition of castle fortification. But such works were already a thing of the past in northern Italy where angle-pointed bastions built largely of earth had become the norm for fortresses and town walls alike. Both Finnart and Albany must have seen them on their travels, and yet both chose to ignore them.

This is all the more surprising given that the effectiveness of earth as a defence against gunpowder artillery had already been effectively demonstrated in Scotland. In 1523, Lord Dacre attempted to take Cessford (Roxburghshire), the impressive mid-fifteenth-century tower-house castle of Sir Andrew Ker, warden of the East March. Armed to the teeth with three heavy siege guns and eight lighter pieces, Dacre's men spent a whole day toiling without success to seize the place. Dacre's explanation for his failure to take it by force was that the castle was 'vawmewred with earth of the best sort I have seen'; a 'vawmure' being an earthwork raised against a wall-face.

The first hint of the use in Scotland of the earthen, angle-pointed bastion – *trace italienne* as it has become known – comes in the 1540s from Edinburgh Castle. Following the English invasion of 1544, a major scheme of refortification was put in hand there which included the construction of an angular earthwork, later called the Spur, projecting out over Castle Hill, where the Esplanade is today. The engineer responsible may have been the Italian, Migliorino Ubaldini, sent to Scotland by Henri II of France, the future father-in-law of Queen Mary.

It was following a further invasion in September 1547 that the English themselves began to take a closer interest in *trace italienne* fortification, to defend the new garrisons which the duke of Somerset was counting on to consolidate his hold on the country. They had already dabbled in the form, and learnt much through their defence of Boulogne, and in the spring of that year had constructed a modest angle-bastioned work on the Isle of Wight. But it was Scotland that provided the theatre of war in which to test and further perfect the new breed of fortification.

Between Somerset's breathtaking victory over the Scottish host at Pinkie in 1547 and the signing of the Treaty of Boulogne in 1550, by which the English were forced out of 'the boundis of Scotland', the English erected six major garrison fortresses. They reached from Roxburgh, on the Border, to Broughty, on the Firth of Tay, and as far inland as Lauder, in the shadow of the Lammermuir Hills. The others were at Eyemouth on the Berwickshire coast, and at Dunglass and Haddington, both in East Lothian. Alas, nothing survives today of Haddington, the mightiest of them, and scarcely anything of Broughty or Lauder. Only at Dunglass, Roxburgh and Eyemouth are there now significant remains.

65 The caponier in the great ditch at Craignethan Castle, as excavated in 1964.

66 An impression of the Craignethan caponier being used in 1540 (Harry Bland).

All shared the same technique of fortification. The basic principle was a reliance on enormously thick earthen ramparts, which would soak up the incoming artillery shot, augmented by arrowhead-shaped bastions projecting into the field. A careful attention to geometry ensured that every face, whether on bastion or rampart, was 'covered' by another part of the fortification. Stone was hardly used, being restricted to the outer faces of the ramparts and bastions and the bases of the gun-platforms, as excavations at Eyemouth recently showed.

Eyemouth was the first to be built, over the winter of 1547–8; this was one of the attractions of *trace italienne* works, they were quick, and comparatively inexpensive, to build (**67**). Sir Richard Lee's design centred on a single bastion midway along a 15m (50ft)-thick rampart cutting off the promontory. Gun-flankers behind the bastion protected the two faces of the rampart, and a broad, flat-bottomed ditch ran in front of all. The bastioned rampart, armed by late 1549 with about ten guns, protected a garrison which was never large, the normal complement consisting of the captain, several lieutenants, a master gunner, two porters, a drummer, surgeon, ensign and clerk plus ten light-horsemen and thirty-four hackbutters.

There was one significant flaw in Lee's original design; the faces of the bastion were not 'covered' by flanking fire from the rampart. These 'blind spots' were only overcome by inserting gun-emplacements in the rampart, thereby weakening the rampart itself. Why Lee opted for a single, central bastion, rather than two bastions, one at each end of the rampart, which would have solved the problem, can only be put down to his incomplete grasp of the principles of the new fortification. Interestingly, when the French reoccupied the fortress in 1557, they abandoned Lee's earlier defence and built just that, a rampart with two terminal angle-bastions immediately in front of it.

In the event, the English fortresses failed to advance Edward VI's cause, just as the great peels built for his namesake two centuries earlier had failed. But none of Somerset's fortresses was found wanting when put to the test; not even the full might of the Franco-Scottish alliance could dislodge the English from their greatest achievement, Haddington. They might have been short-lived affairs, but the lessons learnt were long-lasting. Sir Richard Lee went on to create the mighty fortifications we see today at Berwick-upon-

67 Eyemouth Fort, Berwickshire, from the north east. Lee's arrow-headed bastioned rampart, built in 1547–8, is clearly visible cutting off the narrowest part of the neck of the promontory. Less distinct is the rampart constructed by the French in 1557 beyond Lee's work (that is, towards where the caravan park is now). This had a bastion at either end. The garrison buildings of both forces lay on the grassy headland itself.

Tweed, and over a century later another 'protector', Oliver Cromwell, looked to angle-bastioned forts to help him achieve his goal. And just as Scotland lays claim to having in Eyemouth the first Italianate fortress built in Great Britain, so it can also boast of having the best in Fort George (Inverness-shire), the mighty garrison fortress built in the aftermath of Culloden, the battle fought on a windswept moor close by in 1746. (*Fortress Scotland and the Jacobites*, a companion volume in this series, examines these later military structures.)

Castles and cannon

Blockhouses, gun towers, caponiers and angle bastions, for exclusive use by gunners, were confined to royal castles, coastal defences and garrison fortresses. Only Craignethan was exceptional, just like its creator, for no other lordly residence of the sixteenth century, other than Tantallon, included an artillery fortification *per se* in its construction. But the majority of castles built from the 1560s onwards incorporated horizontal gunholes of one form or another somewhere in their walls.

68 William Forbes' attractive gatehouse at Tolquhon Castle, near Tarves, Aberdeenshire, with its fancy gunholes, grilled windows, sculptured figures and armorial panels. The gatehouse was surely designed more to impress than to deter.

As a rule, these could be counted on the fingers of one hand, and might be randomly scattered about the building. Most were located on the ground floor, often positioned close to an entrance. Their design also varied: as well as the round-ended type found at Dunbar, there were plain rectangular ones, ones with stepped outer splays to stop bullets from ricocheting into the throat, and some very fancy ones. Towards the end of the century, smaller gunholes placed beneath the sills of upper-floor windows started to appear, as well as little shotholes, for use with pistols.

Most gunholes were intended to be used to ward off undesirable intruders – as William Forbes, of Corse Castle (Aberdeenshire), allegedly vowed in 1581: 'I will build me such a house as thieves will need to knock at ere they enter.' They were certainly not capable of withstanding a more determined attack. As with most other aspects of castle design, their appearance was probably as much to do with aesthetic considerations as defensive ones. The attractive triplet-gunholes adorning the gatehouse façade of William Forbes' seat at Tolquhon Castle (Aberdeenshire), built in

69 *St Andrews Castle, Fife.*

70 *The rock-cut mine in St Andrews Castle, dug by the attacking force during the siege of 1546–7.*

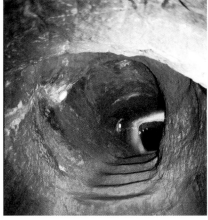

the 1580s, can only have been for show; there was no way they could practically be used with the guns he had cast at the same time (**68**). And the little shotholes visible on the outside of the turrets at Fairnilee (Selkirkshire), a seat of the Ker family built about 1600, do not even penetrate through to the inside!

St Andrews – a castle under siege

Most castles and fortified homes, if they were subjected to attack at all, would have witnessed only lightly armed assaults. Only the major royal and baronial castles were subjected to more fully pressed sieges, such as at Tantallon in 1528, and then only occasionally. One of the most bitterly contested was the assault on St Andrews Castle in 1546–7 which dragged on for fourteen months (**69**). That siege has left evidence of itself in one of the most remarkable examples of siege engineering to survive anywhere in Europe – the mine and countermine (**70**).

The siege began in May 1546 following the assassination of its lord, Cardinal Beaton (**71**), and the occupation of the castle by his assassins, a band of Fife lairds and Protestant sympathizers. By this date the episcopal residence was a formidable stronghold, for not only were the two flanking gun-towers mentioned on page 81 in place, but the cardinal himself had also carried out further strengthening works, chiefly the substantial thickening of the frontal wall. These works contrived to thwart Regent Arran's attempts to take the place by artillery bombardment; other measures were required.

In November, the French ambassador in London reported that Arran's men were digging a mine beneath the castle walls in an attempt to force an entry. The defenders, he noted, were attempting to forestall them by counter-mining. The fruits of their endeavours, filled in immediately after the siege ended, were rediscovered in 1879 and are there for all to see. The mine was a spacious stepped corridor, high and wide enough for pack animals to be used in it to remove the rock more speedily. Surprisingly, the entrance to the mine was situated within 40m (130ft) of the castle walls, demonstrating just how close-fought medieval siege warfare was, even at this late date and well into the era of gunpowder artillery.

The countermine, by contrast, was a cramped affair, testifying to the desperation of the defenders, who by now included John Knox, the fiery Protestant preacher. In fact, they made two false starts in their attempt to locate the mine before succeeding in breaking through. Eventually, the stout defence was broken only when a heavily armed French force arrived and opened up a murderous artillery bombardment. The castle walls were ripped apart. An eyewitness described the devastation: 'Thate daye thai schote downe all the battellyne and caiphouse of the seytowre; and all this daye tha schote upone the easte parte of the castell ... at the hall and chapell, and dislogid us of that parte be downputting of the ruffis and sklatis.' The proof of that statement is evident in the present remains.

More tall storeys

In the meanwhile, life went on. The horrors of the 1540s might lead us into getting things out of proportion and thinking that castle life during the century was one long round of fighting. In this we would be mistaken. For most folk, with the exception perhaps of those on the English Border, life generally would have been reasonably peaceful, interrupted only now and then by the noise of unfriendly voices and the sound of guns. The castles built during the century are testimony to this.

In the 1509 charter granted to Sir John Grant of Freuchie, binding him to carry out defensive works to Urquhart Castle, is an outline also of the kind of residence he was expected to build. He was 'to construct within the castle a hall, chamber, and kitchen, with all the requisite offices, such as pantry, bakehouse, brewhouse, oxhouse, kiln, cot, dovegrove and orchard, with the necessary wooden fences'. This conjures up in the mind's eye a respectable, and peaceful, country seat, albeit one sheltering behind a stout defence. An inventory of the contents, taken in 1545, adds to our understanding of the castle as residence, with its list of beds, feather beds, bolsters, blankets and sheets, tables, chairs and forms, pots and pans, a chest containing 300 pounds, a brew-cauldron, fire-spits, barrels of oats, and three big boats.

The focal point of John Grant's rebuilt castle was the tall tower house that still

71 Cardinal David Beaton; a portrait on display in Arbroath Abbey, one of his numerous benefices.

dominates the skyline (**72**). By now the tower house was the recognized form of lordly residence, adopted at all levels of the landholding class. The new century saw further substantial developments to its layout and detailed design, though it was only with the tower-house boom following the Reformation in 1560 that the most licence was taken.

Edzell Castle – a case study

Typical of the tower-house castles of the first half of the century was Edzell (Angus), the charming residence of the 'lichtsome (carefree) Lindsays' in Glenesk, north of Brechin. It centred on a four-storey L-plan tower house built at one corner of a rectangular barmkin, or courtyard, formed by a defensible wall of middling strength (**73**). The internal arrangement of the tower house followed the pattern of previous centuries, but the entrance into the tower house was now firmly rooted at ground level, where it was 'covered' by a gunhole in the projecting staircase wing. At the wall-top was an attractive parapet rising from a double row of corbels arranged in a chequer pattern – very fashionable throughout the century – with turrets at each angle and in

the middle of each length of wall-walk. Beside the tower house stood a rectangular, two-storey range, which incorporated the main entrance into the courtyard at ground level and a suite of rooms on the upper floor (**74**).

The relationship between the tower house and the adjacent range is now impossible to determine. That the two were constructed at different times, the tower house in the 1530s and the extension in 1553, has led to the view that the tower house was very soon perceived as being too cramped and awkward to live in, requiring a more suitably dignified apartment to be built alongside it. This may have been the case, and the fact that for a short time in the middle of the century Edzell came to be held by the head of the Lindsays, the earl of Crawford himself, is one possible reason for the new building.

But there is too the possibility that the tower house and its adjacent range were planned to co-exist from the outset, to form part of an integral unit, but that there was a pause between the two building operations. Bearing in mind the obligations and size of household of the Lindsays, it is certainly very difficult to see the tower house by itself functioning adequately as a noble residence. Possible confirmation that this may have indeed been the case comes from nearby Melgund Castle.

Edzell and Melgund castles compared

Melgund, near Aberlemno (Angus), was built by Cardinal Beaton (see **71**), the cleric murdered in his official residence, St Andrews, in 1546; his arms and initials, together with those of his mistress, Margaret Ogilvie, occur in several places. The appearance of the castle is very like Edzell's, a tall tower house with a two-storey range attached. But whereas Edzell's development is clearly a staged affair, as the risband (vertical) joints in the outer walls clearly show, Melgund was built all of one piece, a fact recently confirmed by an analysis of the many masons' marks in the fabric.

The distribution of those marks offers a nice insight into how building works might have progressed. Construction work seems to have begun with the tower house, for some of the masons who worked on the ground floor of the hall block only joined the job once the tower house was up to first-floor level. Thereafter, work continued simultaneously on the upper part of the tower house and the central part of the hall block, before the masons moved on to complete the rest of the hall block furthest from the tower house.

The arrangement of the accommodation is clearer at Melgund than at Edzell (**75**). It comprised the lord's private lodging in the tower house, a great hall in the centre of the adjacent range with a withdrawing room at the far end. The architect of Melgund, therefore, managed to create a fully integrated lordly residence where

73 The tower house at Edzell Castle, Angus, built in the 1530s by the Lindsays as their private residence. The fragrant walled garden was added in 1604.

74 The entrance front of Edzell Castle as it might have looked in 1600. The tower house is at the right-hand end. (David Simon).

the public and private elements were brought together under the one roof. Edzell, which shared some of the Melgund masons, seems to have achieved that only in stages. A plausible conclusion, from a study of the masons' marks, is that Edzell's tower house was completed in its entirety in the late 1530s, at which point the masons moved to Melgund. There, they carried through the whole project, before returning once more to Edzell to complete the hall block in 1553. That would suggest that Melgund was completed within ten years.

Beaton's baronial household

Cardinal Beaton built Melgund not for himself but for his eldest natural son, David. The cardinal himself resided elsewhere in a number of residences, including the abbot's house at Arbroath Abbey, the bishop's castle in St Andrews (following his elevation to the archbishopric of St Andrews in 1539), on the episcopal manor at Monimail, also in Fife, and in his lodgings in Edinburgh, at the corner of Blackfriars' Wynd and Cowgate. By the time he succeeded his uncle, James Beaton, as primate of Scotland, he was already at the pinnacle of his career, ruling 'a kingdom within a kingdom', and his household was that of a great nobleman. Wherever his grace was, there was his household, or a considerable part of it, attending to all his needs, both professional and personal. The numbers might not have been quite as large as those serving a great thirteenth-century magnate, like Walter Moray of Bothwell, but they would still have been substantial, and they all required to be housed somewhere.

Beaton's household consisted on the one hand of his professional *familia*, his group of experienced administrators, secretaries and clerks, and on the other of his personal officials and servants. The former was largely composed of relatives and friends from his upbringing in the East Neuk of Fife. They were all people whom he could trust. George Durie, his cousin, abbot of Dunfermline and archdeacon of St Andrews, was scarcely out of his company and the most frequent witness of his master's writs. Bernard Bailie, a distant relation, and parson of Lamington, in Clydesdale, became his closest friend and curator of the young laird of Melgund. The two spent much of their time in their master's company, but they had their own residences to which they would have retired from time to time.

His personal staff, though, would have been permanently bound to their master's side. The most trusted was John Beaton of Balfour, his nephew, who was captain of St Andrews Castle; under him were the small army of guards, men-at-arms and gunners (**76**). Then there was his private writing office, headed by another nephew, John

Lauder, and his colleague, Andrew Oliphant, Beaton's 'weel belovit clerk'; his two chaplains, who looked after his private chapel, and two almoners, who looked after the needy at the castle gate; his master of works, who had charge of the masons, barrowmen, smiths and wrights working on refortifying the castle during much of the cardinal's episcopacy; his provisor, who victualled the castle with food and drink; the master of his household, with his 'army' of cooks and kitchen staff, including the keeper of the pewter; the master of the horse and his stable hands; the minstrels, upholsterers, baker, brewer and gardeners and a host of personal attendants, pages, lackeys, tailors, barber and apothecary. As if that wasn't enough, there were about another twenty assorted servants, including his fool. Other than the 'high heid yins', most of the lower-ranking servants remain nameless in the records. However, we do know that the unfortunate castle porter, killed on the same day as his master, was Ambrose Stirling, that Gabriel, the cook, and Claud, the barber, were French, and that the poor fool went by the name of John Lowys.

Huntly Castle and the noble life

Very little remains now of Cardinal Beaton's residence in St Andrews Castle. It was so badly damaged during the siege that followed his death that it makes it very difficult for us to envisage how his enormous household was accommodated. We therefore have to look elsewhere, to a castle that has survived relatively complete, which was built about 1550, and by a nobleman of similar standing to Beaton. We have the perfect castle in Huntly (**77**).

The origins of Huntly Castle go back to the twelfth century, to the time of Earl Duncan of Fife, who built a motte-and-bailey castle in this beautiful setting beside the River Deveron. During the fourteenth century, the castle passed into the hands of the Gordons, a Berwickshire family that had loyally served Bruce. They were not long in climbing up the social ladder and by 1449 the head of the house was first earl

76 The statue of a crossbowman high up on the palace in Stirling Castle, built around 1540.

77 Huntly Castle, Aberdeenshire, from the north east. In the background is a glimpse of the grassy mound of the original motte (late twelfth century), and in the foreground the unfinished early seventeenth-century east range. In the centre, dominating everything, is the palace, the 'new expensive stately building' erected by the fourth earl of Huntly, and modified by his grandson, the first marquis.

of Huntly. In 1547, a year after Beaton's murder, George Gordon, the fourth earl, was appointed lord chancellor of Scotland, and his elevation to one of the highest offices of State prompted him to erect a 'new expensive stately building, which he had joined to the old castle and rendered a very convenient place'. The new residence was ready in time for the visit in 1556 of Marie of Guise, now the queen-regent.

The reception Marie received was magnificent. She was welcomed at the castle gates by a guard of honour of 1,000 men, and the splendour of her entertainment was such that, after a few days, she wished to depart so as to relieve the burden on her host. Huntly assured her that his cheer was within his means and astonished her by displaying the spacious vaults crammed with provisions. Those vaults survive yet, as does much of the rest of the earl's residence, and despite the alterations that were subsequently made to the place, it is perfectly possible to picture it at the time of the queen's visit.

The 'old castle' mentioned above was the L-plan tower house that now exists as foundations only; it was blown up during a siege by James VI in 1594. Little more can be said about it except that it was probably built about 1400, to serve as the lordly apartment within the castle, but that by the time of the royal visit, had been downgraded to provide accommodation for senior members of the earl's household and their servants.

The earl's residence was now relocated in the 'new expensive stately building', known today as 'the palace'. It was oblong on plan with a large, round tower projecting from one corner (**78**). Such projecting towers were once thought to have been built primarily for defensive reasons, to 'cover' adjacent walls (there were similar round towers added at Edzell and Melgund), and the existence of two wide-mouthed gunholes in the tower at Huntly gives some credence to this. But the motivation may have had more to do with show than strength. Such impressive round towers, housing the noble family's most important accommodation, may have been inspired by French donjons prominent at, for example, Marie of Guise's family seats of Joinville and Nancy. In an earlier chapter, we saw how the great donjon at Coucy might well have inspired a previous generation of Scots. Certainly, under Marie of Guise, French influence at the Scottish court had never been so strong in a long while.

The lowest of the five storeys was given over to three storage cellars in the main block and a grim prison in the basement of the round tower. On the first floor in the main block was a kitchen flanked by two cellars, conceivably the pantry (from the

French *paneterie*, bread store) and buttery, or wine cellar (from the French *bouteillerie*, bottle store). The room in the adjacent tower, above the prison, was probably the steward's chamber, for it was well lit, had a fireplace and a latrine closet, and, crucially, two back-stairs giving access to the earl's suite of rooms on the floor above.

The earl's apartment comprised three rooms, two of which are referred to in a document dated 1576. One was called 'the grit chalmer' (great chamber), also referred to as the 'chalmer of daice (dais)', and the other 'his owin chalmer . . . quhilk . . . was ane round within (that is, beyond) the grit chalmer'. The third room, we may presume, was the earl's hall. This was the conventional arrangement of the day. All three were reception rooms, graded according to the rank of those being received. The hall, the largest in size, was the least restricted of the rooms and served also as dining room; the great chamber was a more

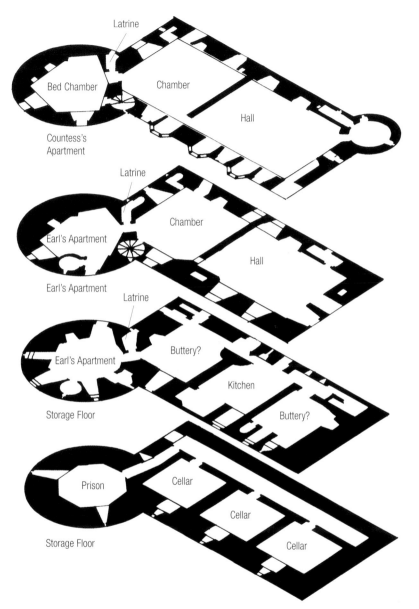

intimate room, the ancestor of the drawing room; the inner chamber in the large, round tower was the earl's bedchamber. Between the great and inner chambers was the earl's latrine closet.

The floor above the earl's apartment was identical in plan, with a sequence of three rooms, and was presumably the countess's suite, for the two leading persons in

78 *Floor plans of the palace at Huntly Castle.*

the castle had separate households. The purpose of the remaining accommodation in the palace is unclear, but the garret may have contained ancillary bedchambers, and there must surely have been a private chapel, perhaps in the range to the east.

We know from an inventory taken after the earl of Huntly's fall from grace in 1562 that the palace rooms presented a most impressive picture of wealth and splendour; among the treasures was the silk tent in which Edward II had slept the night before Bannockburn. The rooms themselves had plastered walls draped with tapestries and other embroidered hangings. Most of the floors were covered with woven rush mats, the oriental carpets then becoming fashionable being reserved as ornamental table-covers. Furniture was sparse; apart from the chair and canopy of estate in the earl's great chamber, and the richly hung beds, the main pieces were trestle-tables, forms and stools, and chests for storing tableware, linen, furnishings and valuables. A sixteenth-century nobleman's life was still largely peripatetic.

There is one aspect of the noble life that intrigues me: who slept where when the monarch came to stay? Marie of Guise and her entourage must surely have taken precedence over everyone else, including the earl and countess, during her stay in 1556. Did this mean that the earl vacated his apartment in deference to his superior? And if so, did he then displace the countess from her apartment? And if so, whom did she displace? Perhaps it is just as well that there are certain aspects of noble life that we remain ignorant of.

The post-Reformation tower house

The silk tent of Edward II stored at Huntly Castle was part of a treasure-house of riches spirited away from Aberdeen Cathedral in 1559, in anticipation of trouble ahead. It was not long in coming. In the following year, the Reformation parliament officially recognized the end of Catholicism and the adoption of Protestantism as the nation's religion.

This watershed in Scottish history heralded another castle-building boom. But why? The redistribution of Church lands and property into the hands of secular lords after 1560 has traditionally been given as the spur, but in truth this material change had happened a generation and more before 1560, for example with the transfer of monastic estates into lay benefices. David Beaton himself effectively held Arbroath Abbey as a private estate after becoming archbishop of St Andrews in 1539.

Perhaps the more likely reason for the building boom was the rising esteem that the lesser lairds, those below the rank of lords of parliament, were attaining during this momentous period of change in Scottish society. Certainly, by 1560, they had flexed their muscles to the extent that one hundred of them had won the right to sit in the Reformation parliament for the first time. And in its aftermath, these same lairds were to take a much more active role in the organization of the new Church, which was to become more parish-based. These 'bonnet lairds' were the ones who contributed most to the new boom.

The plethora of fortified houses, chiefly tower houses, built after 1560 has been contrasted with the comparative dearth of castle building throughout the first half of the century, and the phrase 'the long pause' has been coined to describe this relative barrenness. However, we need to be more cautious about depicting the period up to the Reformation as a half-century of dearth in castle construction. We have seen above something of the quality of work underway in Angus between the 1530s and 1550s, and other areas of the country show similar activity. We must also be alert to the possibility that some of the post-Reformation tower houses may simply be a refurbishment of an existing building.

The lesson of Carsluith Castle (Kirkcudbrightshire) is salutary (**79**). At first sight it looks for all the world like a late sixteenth-century L-plan tower house, and the date in the armorial panel over the front door, now almost illegible but recorded previously as 1568, confirms that view. However, a closer inspection of the fabric points to a more complicated building history. It probably began life as a simple oblong tower built about 1500, in which case the acquisition in 1506 of the lands of Carsluith through marriage by Lindsay of Fairgirth may have been the trigger for the new building. The building operation recorded in the armorial stone may simply allude to the remodelling of that building by the new owners, the Brouns.

79 The late sixteenth century L-plan tower house at Carsluith, Kirkcudbrightshire, began life about 1500 as a rectangular building. The projecting jamb was added when the Brouns took possession of the property in the 1560s and decided to mark their arrival in a very visible way.

Notwithstanding this caveat, there is no escaping the fact that castle building after 1560 was prodigious. It affected all parts of the country. Furthermore, the architect-masons responsible for the work took the quite simple forms that had been handed down to them to new and exciting heights of planning and design. They explored a multiplicity of ground plans – Ls, Zs, Es and Ts and variants of these; they made improvements to the quality of life inside the tower; and they exercised considerable ingenuity in the treatment of the exteriors, particularly the wall-head.

80 Claypotts Castle, Angus, built for John Strachan in the aftermath of the Reformation in 1560.

Claypotts – the residence of a bonnet laird

One point worth bearing in mind when looking at the post-Reformation tower house is the likely status of the builder. Normally, a bonnet laird had just one modest estate, with equally modest obligations to go with it. The size of his household was tailored to these needs, and so was his residence. Claypotts, the home near Dundee of the Strachans, is typical of these residences of bonnet lairds (**80**).

At the beginning of the sixteenth century, the Strachans were lay tenants in Claypotts, holding the land from the abbot of Lindores. They also held other small farms nearby from the abbeys of Arbroath and Balmerino. For their principal holding, Claypotts, they paid the abbot a £12 annual rent with twelve cockerels thrown in for good measure. In addition, they were liable to attend the monastic court when required, and in time of war were obliged to provide a quarter of the cost of an armed horseman with an attendant foot soldier. This situation continued up to the Reformation, when the unfortunate monks of Lindores had to endure the sight of their church being wrecked by the Reformers. But, in common with many of their monastic brethren, they were allowed to remain in their cloister for the rest of their days so long as they embraced the new faith – which they did.

The new relationship between John Strachan and the abbot of Lindores spurred the former to embark on a new building, to reflect his newfound status. Within a decade of the Reformation parliament, work had begun on constructing the present building of Claypotts; the date 1569 is carved on the fabric. The tower house was built on the Z-plan, with two round towers projecting from diametrically opposed corners of the main block. Whether this was for reasons of defence or show cannot now be determined. There is no doubting the earnestness of the twelve wide-mouthed gunholes at ground level, or the defensive capability of the two barriers at the entrance, but these features, and others we find on buildings of this date – such as iron grilles over windows (see **68**) and timber drawbars behind doors and window shutters – are the medieval equivalents of today's outside security lights, door-chains and window locks. The Strachans were just as concerned as we are about intruders.

The internal arrangements at Claypotts were broadly similar to those in earlier tower houses, but with important differences. Two or more stairs were now provided – the main (public) stair and the back (service) stair(s) – so that the gentlefolk of the house would not have to rub shoulders with the servants. The sanitary arrangements were also improved, for the draughty open-chuted latrines were now replaced by portable soil boxes, called 'closed stools' (something like the modern chemical toilet) that were emptied as required.

The kitchen was also now an ever-present feature. Hitherto, many tower houses had been without a formal kitchen, because the main room for dining in was the great hall, situated elsewhere in the castle complex. Any cooking done in the tower house would have been done informally over the hall fire. But bonnet lairds did not have the substantial obligations of the senior nobility, like Beaton and Huntly, and so did not need such complex residences. For the first time in the long history of the Scottish castle, we can say of these modest later sixteenth-century tower houses that they were the 'be all and end all' of the lairdly residence, more akin to a private home than a public place of lordship (**81**).

Just in case we are in any doubt as to the relative standing of John Strachan and his like to the Beatons and the Huntlys of that time, a peep into his last will and testament, drawn up in 1593, confirms his modest standing. Three women looked after his house, including Janet Wilkie who had been with the family for fourteen years. Four ploughmen and a shepherd worked his land, and in that year they had 'sawin [sown]' on the ground of Claypotts' 8 bolls of wheat, 50 bolls of oats, 14 bolls of barley and 6 bolls of peas, and tended 79 sheep, 14 oxen, 7 bullocks, 5 cows and 2 workhorses. Add to all this the value of his 'guidis, geir, sowmes of money and dettis perteining' and we have a bonnet laird worth £1,222 6s 8d at his death. This put John Strachan a cut above the average farmer or laird, who was worth little more than £500 at that date. Claypotts Castle was therefore the residence of a farmer of above average means – and it shows.

If Claypotts was at the top end of the scale of residences built by 'bonnet lairds', then Fourmerkland Tower, north of Dumfries, was pretty well near the bottom. Built about 1590 by Robert Maxwell, a relation of the earl of Herries, it was one of the smallest post-Reformation tower houses, with a floor area totalling no more than 70sq m (750sq ft), a third of the size of Claypotts. But everything is relative, and although his modest fortified house may pale into insignificance alongside Claypotts, in terms of his standing in Border society Robert Maxwell was among the top ten per cent of landholders in terms of wealth, with an estate valued at £300 at his death. There were other small-time lairds below him, and their fortified homes reflected this.

Fortified farmhouses on the Border and beyond

In the lonely valley of the Jed Water, 8km (5 miles) south of Jedburgh, and within sight of England, stands the isolated ruin known as Slacks Tower (**82**). Surrounded today by crumbling stone dykes and grazing sheep, Slacks in the late sixteenth century was the throbbing heart of a small farm held by one of the Oliver 'surname', a noted reiving (plundering) family. William Oliver 'of Slakis', the likely builder, took part in a raid in 1583.

The ruin still stands pretty well to roof height and the arrangement of the accommodation is clear enough. The building consisted of two floors and a garret. There was no vault. The ground floor was entered separately through a doorway in the downward-facing gable, originally fitted with two doors, one presumably of timber opening outwards, and the other, an iron yett, opening inwards and further strengthened by a timber drawbar. A second doorway in a side wall, reached from the ground by an outside timber stair, gave access to the upper floors; it was similarly secured. The upper floors had small windows, which is more than the ground floor had, and the main floor was heated from an open hearth with a smoke-hood, or 'hingin' lum', above it. Access to the garret must have been by ladder. Even though the amount of living space (100sq m/1,076sq ft) is greater than that at Fourmerkland, the impression, all in all, is of a rude lairdly dwelling.

It has been said of buildings like Slacks that they were temporary shelters in times of trouble, bolt-holes where their owners, their servants, tenants and possessions could shelter whenever a cross-border raid or internal feud threatened. Normal daily life was lived in the less substantial dwellings of timber and turf placed around the building, and these survive, albeit as foundations only, remarkably well at Slacks (**83**). But I find this picture very hard to credit.

There is no gainsaying the fact that structures like Slacks were used to shelter people and possessions, including livestock, at critical times

82 Slacks Tower, south of Jedburgh, Roxburghshire, from the north east, with the remains of farm buildings around it. The two upper floors, comprising the main accommodation, were entered through a first-floor door in the side wall (where the gap now is). The ground floor was separately accessed through a door in the right-hand gable.

(eight cattle were burnt to death inside William Douglas's farmhouse at Cunzierton (Dumfriesshire) during a raid in 1540). But this does not preclude them from being used as permanent residences. Would Border lairds like the Olivers really have left the best building on their farm unoccupied for a greater part of the time? I doubt it.

There is no getting away from the fact that life on both sides of the Border in the years either side of 1600 was particularly troubled. Reiving and feuding were endemic, law and order conspicuously absent. For families like the Olivers, security was uppermost in their minds. But they would only have built robust buildings like Slacks if they had something worth protecting. When we look on Slacks today, lonely and slowly crumbling before our eyes, it is only too easy to conjure up a picture of a scruffy reiver mucking out the byre by day and raiding over the Border by night. But the truth is that the Olivers and their like had never been wealthier. No matter how they had come by that wealth – and the Olivers took as much as they lost, like any reivers worth their salt – the fact remains that they were comparatively well off and wished to stay that way. Their fortified farmhouses, like Slacks, were just as much outward and visible signs of wealth and status as the mighty baronial castles and fortified towers of their betters, relatively speaking.

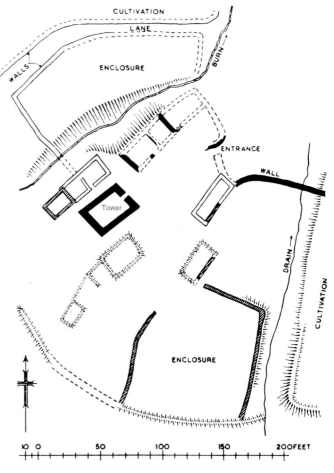

83 Plan of Slacks Tower and farm.

Slacks is one of only a handful of these fortified houses surviving in recognizable condition in the Border country. But they must have been far commoner sights in their heyday between 1560 and 1650, and field survey is adding examples to the list all the time. Among the most remarkable of recent discoveries is the existence of several buildings, similar in most respects to Slacks, far away from the Border, in Upper Clydesdale. Some have been found hiding inside later structures, while others have been discovered lurking in remote valleys in the wilds of the Lowther Hills. Several have been excavated, including those at Glenochar (**84**) and Wintercleuch, both in the parish of Crawford (Lanarkshire). The picture emerging is of structures similar in size to Slacks (that is, with about 100sq m (1,076sq ft) of floor space spread

over two floors and a garret) but with differences in the detail. These include just one entrance doorway, at ground level, a vaulted ground floor with slit openings, and an internal stair. And, like Slacks, they stand at the hearts of larger complexes comprising less substantial buildings, byres and enclosures.

The discovery of a hoard of coins, including several Elizabethan sixpences, beside the building at Glenochar not only confirms the date of construction and initial occupation but also demonstrates that the laird, whoever he was, was a man of means. So who were the lairds responsible for these Clydesdale examples? Surviving wills clearly show that most were tenant farmers who were becoming wealthier due to their growing flocks of sheep and herds of cattle. Recent research has raised the intriguing possibility that a few may have been associated with the prosperous gold and lead workings in the area. Certainly, the lairds at Glendorch (Foulis), Snar (Douglas) and Glengonnar (Bulmer) are known to have been directly involved in the industry. These were men of substance, working 'God's treasure house in Scotland', which, like the Border country, was not without its lawlessness and its share of thieves, murderers and outlaws. The seventeenth century may have dawned, and the king of Scots become the king of England also, but the bonnet lairds of Upper Clydesdale were just as much in need of strong and impressive fortified residences as their predecessors 500 years before.

Epilogue:
a continuing love affair

By any meanes do not take away the battlement . . . for that is the grace of the house, and makes it look lyk a castle.

As late as 1689, the Reverend Thomas Morer, an English chaplain serving with a Scottish regiment, wrote: 'The houses of the gentry are high and strong, and appear more like castles than houses, made of thick stone walls, with iron bars for their windows.' His words had a kernel of truth about them, for it took the Scots a long time to cast off their defensive shells. Indeed, in the early years of the century they were even exporting the idea to Ulster as part of the Jacobean 'plantation' (**85**). Even while Morer was penning his *Short Account*, someone as grand as Archibald Douglas, first earl of Forfar, was still residing within the crumbling medieval walls of Bothwell Castle. Only as the century drew to its close did he set about building a fine new mansion, Bothwell House, a short distance away. He was not alone. Morer observed this trend: 'Yet now they begin to have better buildings, and to be very modish both in the fabrick and furniture of their dwellings: tho' still their avenues are very indifferent and they want their gardens.'

Even among those building anew during the seventeenth century there were still quite a number who stayed faithful to the lofty, tower-house form. They included William 'Danzig Willie' Forbes, at Craigievar Castle (Aberdeenshire), and Sir Alexander Nisbet of that Ilk, at Nisbet House, near Duns (Berwickshire). One

85 Monea Castle, Co. Fermanagh, Ulster, built in 1618 by Malcolm Hamilton, a Lanarkshire gentleman, who settled in Ulster as part of King James VI's 'plantation' and subsequently rose to become archbishop of Cashel. With land in excess of 2000 acres, Hamilton was obliged to build a castle and bawn (the Irish word for a barmkin). The similarity between Monea and Claypotts is striking.

possible explanation for this conservatism is given in Sir Robert Ker's plea of 1632 to his son, William, regarding the rebuilding of his house at Ancrum, near Jedburgh, quoted at the beginning of this chapter. The age when brave retainers manned the battlements and poured boiling oil on the heads of besiegers may have long passed, but crenellations and other castle trappings still served as icons of lordship.

Not that the seventeenth century was all sweetness and light; far from it. James VI, in his dotage, may have boasted: 'This I must say for Scotland, here I sit and govern it with my pen: I write and it is done, and by a clerk of the Council I govern Scotland now, which others could not do by the sword'; but the decades following the Union of the Crowns in 1603 remained troubled ones. Within ten years of Sir Alexander Nisbet building his fortified residence in 1630, and less than three miles away from it on Duns Law, the covenanting army had hastily to erect a bastioned fort from which they could confront Charles I's royalist army. And the earthen ravelins, or gun emplacements, built to protect the likes of Hermitage, Huntly and Tantallon during the civil war that followed, survive to testify to the continuing insecurity. Cromwell's invasion of 1650 and the subsequent ten-year English occupation, followed immediately after by the religious strife of the 1670s and 1680s, continued the uncertainty. Even as late as 1689, during the first Jacobite uprising, castles throughout the Highlands had perforce to become garrisons once more.

But these were the exception rather than the rule. The mighty castles of medieval magnates were now giving way to magnificent mansions like Drumlanrig Castle (Dumfriesshire), begun about 1676 by the first duke of Queensberry and not really a castle at all. And the tower-house castles of the lesser nobility and gentry were gradually being replaced by more modest lairds' houses – lower, smaller, unvaulted, and only very slightly fortified.

But the Scots have never really ceased their love affair with the castle. They might have let many fall into ruin in the eighteenth century, and made good use of the stones and slates elsewhere, but somehow these ancient seats of lordship remained as symbols of power. When, in 1715, John Erskine, earl of Mar, plotted his uprising in support of King James VIII & III, the exiled 'pretender' to the throne of Great Britain and Ireland, it was at his ancestral castle of Kildrummy that he marshalled his forces and from where he embarked on his mission. By the end of the century, ruined castles were becoming compelling features in the landscape. Captain Grose, who sketched so many of them for his *Antiquities of Scotland*, published in 1789, summed up their attraction: 'Let us view the castle of some ancient thane, its hall, its dungeons and embattled towers mantled with ivy.'

This Romantic perception led to a renewed interest in the castle, to the extent that, through the nineteenth century, a considerable number were repaired, to become eye-catching curiosities – and, of course, the stuff of myth and legend. So obsessed were they by the castle that the Scots evolved an architectural style, Scots Baronial, whose debt to the mason-architects of medieval times is self-evident. And the love affair continues to this day, with some even prepared to invest their life-savings in restoring castles, to serve as useful, and impressive, residences once more.

Perched on haughland beside the Gadie Burn, near Insch in Aberdeenshire, is a lovingly restored castle, Leslie (**86**). It was one of the last fortified houses built in Scotland, in 1661. But it was very probably also the site of one of the first, for the lands of 'Lesselyn' were acquired in the twelfth century by Bertolf, a Fleming, whose descendants took the name of Leslie. Appropriately, it was a family bearing the Leslie surname that restored it, and I imagine they were every bit as proud of their castle as their predecessors.

86 *Leslie Castle, near Insch, Aberdeenshire, undergoing restoration in 1984.*

Castles to visit

HS   Historic Scotland
NTS   National Trust for Scotland
LA   Local Authority
P   Private Ownership

Please note that those castles in private ownership are not necessarily readily open to visitors, and permission should be obtained in advance from the owner.

Twelfth-century castles

Aberdour Castle, Fife (HS)

An extensive ruin of the Douglases, illustrating how a medieval castle could be extended and modified over several centuries. The extensive walled and terraced gardens give a good idea of how a castle was much more than just a place to live in.

Bass of Inverurie, Aberdeenshire (LA)

A fine motte-and-bailey castle, built by Earl David of Huntingdon about 1190.

Castle Sween, Argyllshire (HS)

The oldest standing castle in Scotland, built by Suibhne 'the Red', founder of Clan MacSween, in the late twelfth century. A substantial ruin, only marginally altered in later centuries.

Crookston Castle, Glasgow (HS)

Perhaps the best-preserved 'ringwork' castle in Scotland, built by Robert Croc, a vassal of the Stewarts. The imposing tower house was built around 1400 by the Stewarts of Darnley, but badly damaged (perhaps by Mons Meg) in the siege of 1489.

Cubbie Roo's Castle, Orkney (HS)

Probably the earliest stone castle to survive, built about 1145 by the Norseman, Kolbein Hruga. The ruins of a small rectangular tower are enclosed within a circular ditch that has been built over by later structures. Nearby is the ruined twelfth-century St Mary's Church.

Duffus Castle, Morayshire (HS)

The finest motte-and-bailey castle in state care, built by Freskin, a Fleming, about 1150. The stone keep on top of the motte and the walls encircling the bailey date from the early fourteenth century.

Edinburgh Castle, Midlothian (HS)

The most famous Scottish castle, with a history of occupation on the castle rock reaching back to the Bronze Age 3000 years ago. St Margaret's Chapel (twelfth century), the Fore Well (thirteenth century), David's Tower (fourteenth century), the Vaults (fifteenth century) and Great Hall (1511) survive from the Middle Ages. The rest, including the marvellous array of defensive walls, dates from the sixteenth century and later. Mons Meg, one of the finest and earliest medieval cannons, is proudly on display there.

Huntly Castle, Aberdeenshire (HS)

One of the noblest baronial ruins in Scotland. The castle was the chief residence of the Gordon clan, with a history of occupation extending from the twelfth to the seventeenth century. The complex has a fine motte, the foundations of a large fifteenth-century tower house and, the real wonder, an imposing palace dating from the fifteenth century but substantially remodelled in the mid-sixteenth century, and further sumptuously enriched about 1600.

Mote of Urr, Kirkcudbrightshire (P)

The finest motte-and-bailey castle in the country, built by Walter de Berkeley about 1160. Excavation showed that the summit was raised in height following the destruction of the timber buildings in the later twelfth century. It is possible that the 'bailey' dates from an earlier period.

Roxburgh Castle, Roxburghshire (P)

The awesome castle mound and encircling ditch are all that survive of this vitally strategic royal castle, built in the early twelfth century at the confluence of the rivers Tweed and Teviot. The chunks of masonry on the summit date from the English occupation after 1296. The outline of the English garrison fort built in the late 1540s can also be made out.

Stirling Castle, Stirlingshire (HS)

A marvellous array of late medieval buildings crowns the summit of the castle rock which overshadows two of the great battlefields in Scottish history – Stirling Bridge in 1297 and Bannockburn in 1314. Pride of place are James IV's Great Hall (recently restored) and James V's Palace.

Thirteenth–century castles

Balvenie Castle, Banffshire. (HS)

A curtain-walled castle of the Comyns, remodelled by the Black Douglases in the fifteenth century, and with a new lodging added by the fourth earl of Atholl about 1550. The double-leafed iron yett in the entrance gateway is most unusual.

Bothwell Castle, Lanarkshire (HS)

One of the outstanding monuments of medieval Scotland. Its mighty thirteenth-century donjon is undoubtedly the finest castle fragment surviving in the country. The rebuilding by the Black Douglases, after the wars with England in the fourteenth century, testifies to their lofty status in society.

Caerlaverock Castle, Dumfriesshire (HS)

Not one but two castles, both built by the Maxwells. The older one, dating from the 1220s, was abandoned in the 1270s and replaced by the present castle, one of the most attractive in the country. Besieged by Edward I of England in 1300, it was largely rebuilt after the wars of independence, and continued as the Maxwells' chief residence until 1640. The interior has a splendid Renaissance range dating from the 1630s.

Castle Tioram, Argyllshire (P)

A lonely and evocative ruin, perched on a rocky island at the head of Loch Moidart, built by the chief of Clan MacRuari. The thirteenth-century curtain wall has fine original features; the tower and other internal buildings date from the fourteenth century and later.

Dirleton Castle, East Lothian (HS)

A formidable fortress built about 1240 for the de Vauxs. Much of their castle survives, despite major refurbishment by the Halyburtons in the later fourteenth century, and the Ruthvens in the later sixteenth century.

Drum Castle, Aberdeenshire (NTS)

Built round one of the oldest tower houses in Scotland, this fine castle has a seventeenth-century range and additions by William Burn in 1875.

Duart Castle, Argyllshire (P)

A fine curtain-walled castle of the MacLeans, with a tower house added in the fourteenth century, and other ranges later. The ruin was restored early last century.

Dunstaffnage Castle, Argyllshire (HS)

An impressive curtain-walled castle of the MacDougalls, lords of Lorn, overlooking one of the most important sea-lanes on the western seaboard. Recent excavation shows that the projecting towers were added later in the thirteenth century. A fine thirteenth-century castle chapel stands close by.

Dunvegan Castle, Skye, Inverness-shire (P)

Ancestral seat of Clan MacLeod, this is the most famous of all the castles in the Hebrides. The castle is the longest continuously occupied residence in Scotland. Substantial remains of the medieval curtain-walled castle survive despite the extensive remodelling in Georgian times.

Hailes Castle, East Lothian (HS)

A beautifully sited ruin by the River Tyne incorporating a thirteenth-century fortified manor of the de Gourlays. Substantially remodelled by the Hepburns as a tower-house castle from the later fourteenth century, it was a residence of the fourth earl of Bothwell, Mary Queen of Scots' third husband.

Inverlochy Castle, Inverness-shire (HS)

A well-preserved curtain-walled castle of about 1280, built by the Comyns, lords of Lochaber. The largest of the four towers was the donjon, or keep. The place last saw action during the civil war of the 1640s.

Kildrummy Castle, Aberdeenshire (HS)

A substantial ruined curtain-wall castle of the earls of Mar, with projecting towers, great hall and chapel. The gatehouse may be a legacy of Edward I of England's attempted conquest of Scotland. Scene of a great siege in 1306 in which Neil Bruce, Robert the Bruce's brother, was captured. The 1715 Jacobite Rising began here.

Lochranza Castle, Arran, Ayrshire (HS)

Entombed within the later medieval tower house are the remains of a two-storey hall house, built by the MacSweens of Knapdale.

Peel Ring of Lumphanan, Aberdeenshire (HS)

An earthwork-and-timber castle, built about 1250 by the Durwards, lords of nearby Coull Castle, possibly as a hunting-lodge. King Macbeth was killed in the vicinity in 1057.

Rothesay Castle, Buteshire (HS)

A remarkable curtain-walled castle, circular in plan, built by the High Stewart about 1200. Besieged by the Norse in 1230 and again in 1263, it was subsequently strengthened by the addition of four projecting towers. The large forework projecting into the water-filled moat was built by James IV about 1500.

St Andrews Castle, Fife (HS)

The ruins of the archbishop's residence originate in the thirteenth century, but the devastating artillery bombardment during the 1546–7 siege that followed Cardinal Beaton's murder there took its toll. Surviving features include the mine and countermine tunnelled during the siege, and the grisly 'bottle dungeon'.

Skipness Castle, Argyllshire (HS)

This modest hall castle of the early thirteenth century was rebuilt as a substantial curtain-walled castle at the end of the century when the Stewart earls of Menteith wrested the place from the MacSween lords of Knapdale. The Campbells added the impressive tower house in the early sixteenth century. The castle chapel stands near by.

Urquhart Castle, Inverness-shire (HS)

A large, sprawling castle majestically sited on the banks of Loch Ness. Originally built by the Durwards, it figured prominently in the wars of independence, and during the bitter struggle between the Scottish crown and the MacDonald Lords of the Isles that followed. Most of the existing ruin, including the lofty tower house, dates from after 1509 when the castle passed into the hands of the Grants of Freuchie (now Grantown-on-Spey).

Fourteenth–century castles

Doune Castle, Stirlingshire (HS)

Built late in the century for Regent Albany, Robert III's brother and known as Scotland's 'uncrowned king', this large and powerfully impressive courtyard castle has a fine tower house and great hall, restored in the 1880s.

Dundonald Castle, Ayrshire (HS/LA)

The great hilltop tower house was built about 1370 by Robert II, the first Stewart monarch. Excavations have confirmed the existence of a large late thirteenth-century curtain-walled castle and uncovered evidence of occupation reaching back to the Neolithic period.

Glamis Castle, Angus (P)

The original tower house built by the Lyons has been greatly altered and extended over the centuries, but the castle still retains its imposing medieval grandeur.

Hermitage Castle, Roxburghshire (HS)

A vast and eerie ruin in a lonely situation in deepest Liddesdale, 'the bloodiest valley in Britain'. Much restored in the nineteenth century, it incorporates elements from the manor house of the Dacres (about 1350) and substantial portions of the unusual tower house built by William, first earl of Douglas. The complex of earthworks has never been excavated and is therefore a mystery. Nearby is Hermitage Chapel, also fourteenth-century.

Lochleven Castle, Kinross-shire (HS)

Attractively set on an island in the loch, the curtain-walled enclosure is dominated by a rectangular tower house, altered in the sixteenth century and used to imprison Mary Queen of Scots in 1567–8.

Morton Castle, Dumfriesshire (HS)

A dramatically sited, but enigmatic, ruin of a hall-house castle, probably built by one of the Randolphs but later passed to the Douglases.

Neidpath Castle, Peeblesshire (P)

Dramatically sited beside the River Tweed, this large L-plan tower house was built towards the end of the century by the Hay family. Much of the interior was remodelled during the sixteenth and seventeenth centuries but there are many fine features from the original building still to be seen.

Spynie Palace, Morayshire (HS)

The best-preserved medieval bishop's palace in Scotland. The ruins of a fourteenth-century hall-block are overshadowed by the towering mass of the fifteenth-century David's Tower (after Bishop David Stewart 1462-76), the largest tower house in Scotland.

Tantallon Castle, East Lothian (HS)

A remarkable red sandstone fortress residence perched on a promontory overlooking the North Sea. Built by William, first earl of Douglas, about 1350, it was badly damaged by James V's artillery in 1528 and refortified using green stone. The outworks contain important siege works, including a seventeenth-century ravelin (gun battery).

Threave Castle, Kirkcudbrightshire (HS)

The massive tower house was built by Archibald 'the Grim', third earl of Douglas and lord of Galloway, about 1370. Excavations on the island have shown that this was but the central part of a much bigger complex of buildings. The unique artillery fortification was built before the great siege of 1455, that resulted in the downfall of the mighty Black Douglases.

Fifteenth-century castles

Alloa Tower, Clackmannanshire (P)

A fine tower house, built by the Erskines (later earls of Mar), but later modified. Recently restored and open to the public.

Blackness Castle, West Lothian (HS)

Built in the 1440s and massively strengthened by Sir James Hamilton of Finnart (see Craignethan) for James V in the 1530s as an artillery fortress. Used for much of its life as a state prison (one inmate was Cardinal Beaton) and garrison fort.

Borthwick Castle, Midlothian (P)

One of the most impressive tower houses, and certainly one of the largest, built by Sir William (later Lord) Borthwick about 1420. Built on the E plan (without the central stem), it accommodated all the residential and service needs of a nobleman under one roof. The great hall is particularly splendid.

Cardoness Castle, Kirkcudbrightshire (HS)

A well-preserved tower house built by the McCullochs, a powerful Gallovidian family. The outer walls have good, early examples of gunholes, and the interior has high quality carved fireplaces and aumbries.

Castle Campbell, Clackmannanshire (HS)

Formerly called Castle Gloom, this romantically situated castle, flanked by the Burn of Care and the Burn of Sorrow, was adopted by the Campbell earls of Argyll as their Lowland seat (their chief seat being at Inveraray, Argyllshire). A separate hall block complements the tower house, and there are fine seventeenth-century features, including an unusual loggia.

Craigmillar Castle, Midlothian (HS)

The L-plan tower house of about 1400 stands within a curtain wall with a grand machicolated parapet. The ranges around the courtyard date from the sixteenth and seventeenth centuries. A fishpond in the pleasance, or pleasure garden, to the south of the castle forms the letter P for the Prestons, who held the estate for much of its existence.

Crichton Castle, Midlothian (HS)

A large and sophisticated castle, originating about 1400 as a tower house and great hall but greatly enlarged by Chancellor Crichton in the 1440s to become a courtyard castle. The most spectacular part, however, is the range erected by Francis Stewart, fifth earl of Bothwell, in the 1580s, which has a most extraordinary Italianate diamond-faceted courtyard facade and the first scale-and-platt stair built in Scotland.

Dean Castle, Ayrshire (LA)

A tower-house castle of the Boyds, added to in the seventeenth century and nicely restored early in the twentieth century. The fifteenth-century tower now houses impressive collections of armour and musical instruments.

Dunnottar Castle, Kincardineshire (P)

The ancestral seat of the Keiths, the earls marischal, and surely one of the most impressively sited castles anywhere. The oldest structure on the promontory is the L-plan tower house of the early fifteenth century; the remainder of the structures are of the later sixteenth and seventeenth centuries. The Honours of Scotland, the country's crown jewels, were hidden here in the 1650s, during the Cromwellian interlude.

Huntingtower Castle, Perthshire (HS)

Two fine tower houses, built only 3m (10ft) apart, were eventually incorporated into one grand building in the seventeenth century. The interior contains rare sixteenth-century painted walls and ceilings.

Kilchurn Castle, Argyllshire (HS)

A picturesque castle at the head of Loch Awe, built about 1450 by the Campbells of Glenorchy (later earls of Breadalbane). Altered in the 1690s to provide barrack accommodation for the earl's private army.

Kisimul Castle, Barra, Western Isles (HS)

The island home of the MacNeils of Barra, consisting of an irregular curtain wall dominated by a tower house. It was restored after the Second World War.

Lennoxlove, East Lothian (P)

Interesting, if somewhat altered, remnant of a large tower house, built by the Maitlands of Lethington (the original name), but entombed within a later recasting. Now the family seat of the Dukes of Hamilton.

Newark Castle, Renfrewshire (HS)

The tower-house castle of the Maxwells was spectacularly transformed in the 1590s by the wicked Patrick Maxwell into a Renaissance mansion. The fifteenth-century tower house, gatehouse and fragment of barmkin wall survive, as well as impressive interiors from the later mansion.

Orchardton Tower, Kirkcudbrightshire (HS)

A charming little tower-house castle, built by the Cairns family. The tower is, uniquely, circular in plan.

Ravenscraig Castle, Fife (HS/LA)

An enigmatic castle, begun by James II shortly before his death in 1460, then continued under the Sinclair earls of Orkney and completed only in the following century. The myth that this was a purpose-built artillery fort must surely be laid to rest. Nevertheless, it has early gunholes of interest.

Rowallan Castle, Ayrshire (HS)

One of the prettiest castles in the country, this residence of the Mures has a ruined fifteenth-century tower house and a roofed sixteenth-century hall block, later altered to form the main residential accommodation. The 'fairytale' twin towers flanking the entrance date from the mid-sixteenth century.

Smailholm Tower, Roxburghshire (HS)

A rectangular tower house and barmkin built by the Pringles, squires of Black Douglas, in the middle of the century. Excavation uncovered an outer hall and chamber to complement the restricted accommodation in the tower, and evidence for a major remodelling by the Scotts (Sir Walter Scott's forebears) after 1640 when the tower was largely replaced by a two-storey house in the courtyard.

Tolquhon Castle, Aberdeenshire (HS)

Built for the Forbes family, Tolquhon has a fifteenth-century tower which was enlarged by William Forbes between 1584 and 1589 with a large mansion round a courtyard. Noted for its highly ornate gatehouse. William Forbes' fine monumental tomb is in the kirkyard in the nearby village of Tarves.

Sixteenth- and seventeenth-century castles

Carnasserie Castle, Argyllshire (HS)

A handsome building, the home of John Carswell, first Protestant bishop of the Isles. The integrated plan of tower house and hall is unusually well preserved, as are many fine architectural details.

Carsluith Castle, Kirkcudbrightshire (HS)

A pretty ruin of a tower house built in the early part of the century but converted by the Brouns into an L-plan tower after 1560. The flanking ranges are eighteenth-century.

Claypotts Castle, Angus (HS)

A most attractive and complete Z-plan tower house, built in the 1570s for the Strachans. The circular towers on the diagonally opposed corners, corbelled out to form overhanging cap houses, give the building its special charm.

Corgarff Castle, Aberdeenshire (HS)

A rectangular tower house in remote Strathdon, built by the Forbeses, but substantially altered by the government after Culloden into barracks for 'redcoats'. The scene of an horrific fire in 1571, the result of a long-standing feud between the Forbeses and Gordons.

Craigievar Castle, Aberdeenshire (NTS)

One of the last tower houses built in Scotland, by the Forbeses around 1625, and certainly among the most picturesque. The magnificent first-floor hall, resplendent in its ornamented plaster coat, is a joy to behold.

Craignethan Castle, Lanarkshire (HS)

A formidable stronghold in an inaccessible situation, typical of its builder, Sir James Hamilton of Finnart. Begun in the 1530s, it was the last noble castle built in Scotland. The crown seized, and partly dismantled, it in 1579. The peculiar caponier, or gunners' hut, in the great ditch was discovered during excavation in 1923.

Crathes Castle, Aberdeenshire (NTS)

A lovely L-plan tower house, with notable painted ceilings, dating from the second half of the century. The fine gardens with great yew hedges belong to the early eighteenth century.

Edzell Castle, Angus (HS)

A lovely castle, the property of the 'lichtsome (carefree) Lindsays', with some very important and unique features. The L-plan tower house of about 1530 was soon joined by a hall range. The stunning and fragrant garden, summerhouse and bathhouse were added by Sir David Lindsay about 1604.

Elcho Castle, Perthshire (HS)

A handsome and complete tower house, with four projecting towers and some interesting internal features. The original wrought-iron window grilles are still in place, as are some of the timber sills for mounting small guns.

Eyemouth Fort, Berwickshire (LA)

Hugging a promontory overlooking the harbour are the grass-grown remains of the English angle-bastioned garrison fortress built in 1547, and of the French-built fortress that superseded it a decade later.

Glenbuchat Castle, Aberdeenshire (HS)

A fine example of a Z-plan tower house, built in 1590. Its last laird, John Gordon, 'Old Glenbucket', was a redoubtable Jacobite.

Glenochar Bastel House, Lanarkshire (P)

The ruin of a fortified farmhouse, built about 1590, and one of a number recently discovered in the Upper Clydesdale area. The excavations have uncovered remains of numerous other dwellings, byres and enclosures, all part of the fermtoun.

Greenknowe Tower, Berwickshire (HS)

A pleasing L-plan tower house built by James Seton in 1581, added to in the following century, but largely restored to its original condition in the 1930s. Has a fine iron yett still in position.

MacLellan's Castle, Kirkcudbrightshire (HS)

An unusual, and unusually large, tower house in the centre of Kirkcudbright, begun by Sir Thomas MacLellan of Bombie about 1577 but never finished. The handsome monumental tomb of Sir Thomas and his second wife, Grissel Maxwell, is in the adjacent Greyfriars' Church.

Muness Castle, Shetland (HS)

The most northerly castle in the British Isles, built by Laurence Bruce in 1598. The rectangular building has round towers at diagonally opposite corners.

Noltland Castle, Orkney (HS)

A fine Z-plan tower house, built between 1560 and 1573 by Gilbert Balfour but never completed. Noted for its extravagant array of gunholes.

Scalloway Castle, Shetland (HS)

A fine tower house built in 1600 for Patrick Stewart, earl of Orkney, who was notorious for his cruelty.

Slacks Tower, Roxburghshire (P)

A rare survival of a fortified farmhouse once common throughout the Border country. Built by the Olivers, a noted reiving family, it is surrounded by a remarkable array of other farm buildings, all surviving as foundations only.

Further reading

Background history

Anderson, J. (ed.) *The Orkneyinga Saga*, Edinburgh, 1873 (reprinted 1990).

Barrow, G. *Kingship and unity: Scotland 1000–1306*, London, 1989.

Dodgshon, Robert *The Age of the Clans*, Edinburgh, 2002.

Donaldson, Gordon *Scotland: James V – James VII*, Edinburgh, 1968.

Duncan, A. *Scotland: the making of the kingdom*, Edinburgh, 1975.

Fraser, G. *The Steel Bonnets*, London, 1971.

Grant, Alexander *Independence and nationhood: Scotland 1306–1469*, London, 1984.

Lynch, Michael *Scotland: a new history*, London, 1991.

Nicholson, Ranald *Scotland: the later Middle Ages*, Edinburgh, 1974.

Tabraham, Chris *The illustrated history of Scotland*, Edinburgh, 2003.

Woolgar, C. *The great household in late medieval England*, London, 1999.

Wormald, Jenny *Court, kirk and community: Scotland 1470–1625*, London, 1981.

Yeoman, Peter *Medieval Scotland*, London, 1995

Scottish castles

A large number of castles are in the care of Historic Scotland, and guidebooks are available for most of them. Detailed descriptions of many more are also to be found in the county *Inventories* of the Royal Commission on the Ancient and Historical Monuments of Scotland and *The Buildings of Scotland* series published by Penguin Books.

Coventry, Martin *The castles of Scotland*, Edinburgh, 1997.

Cruden, Stewart *The Scottish castle*, 3rd edn, Edinburgh, 1981.

Dunbar, John *The architecture of Scotland*, London, 1978.

Dunbar, John *Scottish royal palaces*, Edinburgh, 1999.

Fawcett, Richard *The architectural history of Scotland from the accession of the Stewarts to the Reformation 1371–1560*, Edinburgh, 1994.

Fawcett, Richard *Stirling Castle*, London, 1995.

Howard, Deborah *Scottish architecture from the Reformation to the Restoration 1560–1660*, Edinburgh, 1995.

Lindsay, Maurice *The castles of Scotland*, London, 1986.

MacGibbon, David & Ross, Thomas *The castellated and domestic architecture of Scotland from the twelfth to the eighteenth century*, 5 vols, Edinburgh, 1887–92.

MacIvor, Iain 'Artillery and major places of strength in the Lothians and the East Border, 1513–1542', in Caldwell, David (ed.) *Scottish weapons and fortifications 1100–1800*, Edinburgh, 1981.

MacIvor, Iain *Edinburgh Castle*, London, 1993.

McKean, Charles *The Scottish château*, Stroud, 2001.

MacKenzie, William *The medieval castle in Scotland*, Edinburgh, 1927.

McNeill, Tom *Castles*, London, 1992.

Maxwell-Irving, A. 'Early firearms and their influence on the military and domestic architecture of the Borders', *Proceedings of the Society of Antiquaries of Scotland*, vol. 103, 1970–1.

Merriman, Marcus 'The fortresses in Scotland', in Colvin, H. M. (ed.), *The history of the King's works*, vol. IV, 1485–1660 (part II), London, 1982.

Miket, Roger & Roberts, D. *The mediaeval castles of Skye & Lochalsh*, Portree, 1990.

Pringle, D. 'The houses of the Stewart earls in Orkney and Shetland', *New Orkney Antiquaries Journal*, vol.1, 1999.

Sanderson, Margaret '"Kin, freindis and servandis", the men who worked with Archbishop David Beaton', *Innes Review*, vol. XXV, 1, 1974.

Simpson, W. Douglas *The earldom of Mar*, Aberdeen, 1949.

Simpson, G. & Webster, A. 'Charter evidence and the distribution of mottes in Scotland', *Château Gaillard*, vol. 5, 1970.

Stell, Geoffrey 'Architecture: the changing needs of society', in Brown, Jennifer (ed.) *Scottish society in the fifteenth century,* London, 1977.

Stell, Geoffrey 'Late medieval defences in Scotland', in Caldwell, David (ed.) *Scottish weapons and fortifications 1100–1800,* Edinburgh, 1981.

Stell, Geoffrey 'The Scottish medieval castle: form, function & evolution', in Stringer, K. (ed.) *Essays on the nobility in Scotland,* Edinburgh, 1985.

Tabraham, Chris & Good, George 'The artillery fortification at Threave Castle, Galloway', in Caldwell, David (ed.) *Scottish weapons and fortifications 1100–1800,* Edinburgh, 1981.

Tabraham, Chris 'The Scottish medieval towerhouse as lordly residence in the light of recent excavation', *Proceedings of the Society of Antiquaries of Scotland*, vol. 118, 1988.

Tabraham, Chris & Grove, Doreen *Fortress Scotland and the Jacobites*, London, 1995.

Tranter, Nigel *The fortified house in Scotland,* 5 vols, Edinburgh, 1962.

Yeoman, P. 'Mottes in north-east Scotland', *Scottish Archaeological Review*, vol.5, 1988.

Zeune, Joachim *The last Scottish castles,* Buch am Erlbach, 1992.

Excavation reports

Cannel, J. & Tabraham, Chris 'Excavations at Duffus Castle, Moray', *Proceedings of the Society of Antiquaries of Scotland*, vol. 124, 1994.

Driscoll, S. & Yeoman, P. *Excavations at Edinburgh Castle, 1988–91,* Edinburgh, 1997.

Ewart, Gordon *Cruggleton Castle: report on excavations 1978–1981,* Dumfries, 1985.

Good, George & Tabraham, Chris 'Excavations at Threave Castle, Galloway, 1974–1978', *Medieval Archaeology*, vol. 25, 1981.

Good, George & Tabraham, Chris 'Excavations at Smailholm Tower, Roxburghshire', *Proceedings of the Society of Antiquaries of Scotland*, vol. 118, 1988.

Haggarty, George & Tabraham, Chris 'Excavation of a motte near Roberton, Clydesdale, 1979', *Transactions of the Dumfriesshire and Galloway Natural History and Antiquarian Society*, vol. 57, 1982.

Laing, L. & MacDonald, A. 'Excavations at Lochmaben Castle, Dumfriesshire', *Proceedings of the Society of Antiquaries of Scotland*, vol. 106, 1974–5.

Lewis, J. 'Excavations at St Andrews, Castlecliffe, 1988-90', *Proceedings of the Society of Antiquaries of Scotland*, vol. 126, 1996.

Lewis, J. & Pringle, D. *Spynie Palace and the bishops of Moray: history, architecture and archaeology*, (Society of Antiquaries of Scotland monograph 21), 2002.

MacIvor, I. 'Craignethan Castle: An experiment in artillery fortification', in Apted, M. (ed), *Ancient Monuments and their Interpretation: Essays presented to A J Taylor*, 1977.

MacIvor, I. & Gallagher, D. 'Excavations at Caerlaverock Castle, 1955-66', *Archaeological Journal*, vol. 156 1999.

Murray, H. & Murray, J. 'Excavations at Rattray, Aberdeenshire. A Scottish deserted burgh', *Medieval Archaeology*, vol. 37, 1993.

Murray, N.S. & Talbot, E. J. 'Excavations at the Peel of Lumphanan, Aberdeenshire, 1975–79', *Proceedings of the Society of Antiquaries of Scotland*, vol. 128, 1998.

Yeoman, Peter 'Excavations at Castlehill of Strachan, 1980–81', *Proceedings of the Society of Antiquaries of Scotland*, vol. 114, 1984.

Glossary

ashlar: stone walling of the highest class, with blocks of regular size, perfectly squared, well faced and finely jointed.

barmkin: a stone wall, of middling strength, surrounding a tower-house castle and courtyard (possibly derived from 'barbican').

bastel-house: a fortified stone house, usually with a vaulted ground floor.

bastion: the strongpoint of an artillery fortification, corresponding to a projecting tower of a medieval castle or town wall. All bastions have two faces meeting at an angle, and two flanks that join the faces to the curtain walls.

bombard: an early, large and cumbersome cannon.

bretasche: a covered timber gallery, or hoard, on a castle wall, commanding the wall face below.

caponier: a covered passage across a defensive ditch through which gunners could fire on the attacking force.

casemate: originally a stone-vaulted gun emplacement, but later extended to include accommodation protected from heavy artillery.

corbel: a projection from a wall, supporting some structure.

crannog: a fortified island, generally man-made, in a loch.

crenelle: a notch in a parapet (see also merlon).

donjon: a strong central tower in a castle, usually housing the lord's residence but also serving as the place of last resort for the garrison.

ferm toun: a farm settlement.

feu: the right to the use of the land in return for a stipulated annual payment.

hackbut: an old form of handgun.

hammer beam: a horizontal timber, in place of a tie-beam, at or near the feet of a pair of roof rafters.

jamb: the side of any opening, such as that of a door, window or fireplace.

laigh: the Scots word for 'low' or 'lower'.

machicolation: a permanent stone defence at the top of a castle wall, carried on corbels (see above) with spaces in between through which the defenders could fire on their assailants below.

merlon: the solid part of a parapet between two crenelles (see above).

peel: a timber palisaded enclosure.

putlog: a cross-piece in a timber scaffolding, the inner end resting in a hole (putlog hole) in the wall.

ravelin: a detached triangular artillery work, surrounded by its own ditch, built in front of a curtain wall, generally at the entrance.

reiver: one who thieves or robs.

scale-and-platt stair: a stair with straight flights and landings.

yett: a grilled iron gate, placed either in front of or, more usually, behind a timber entrance door.

Acknowledgements

I am very grateful to those who have helped me with this book: my colleagues David Breeze and Doreen Grove for their invaluable comments, David Simon, Harry Bland and Tom Borthwick for their reconstruction illustrations, and David Henrie and Mike Brooks for their photographs. I am also indebted to the following individuals and institutions for their kind permission to reproduce material: His Grace the Duke of Roxburghe (2), Roger Miket (14), Iain MacIvor (63), Tam Ward (84), Department of the Environment, Northern Ireland (85), John Knight (86), the Pierpoint Morgan Library, New York (11), the Royal Commission on the Ancient and Historical Monuments of Scotland (40, 43, 44 and 83), the City of Carlisle (31), and the Royal Scottish Geographical Society (3). All the remaining illustrations are Crown Copyright: Historic Scotland. I must also thank the many unsung archaeological heroes who have endured the vagaries of the Scottish climate to shed more light on the history of Scotland's castles. Finally, I owe a special debt to the late Stewart Cruden, whose work *The Scottish Castle* remains the standard textbook on the subject, and whose compendious knowledge and infectious enthusiasm for castles rubbed off on so many people, including me.